INSOMNIA

BOB FLAWS

Edited

foulsham

LONDON • NEW YORK • TORONTO • SYDNEY

foulsham

The Publishing House, Bennetts Close, Cippenham,
Slough, Berkshire, SL1 5AP, England

ISBN 0–572–02568-8

Copyright ©1997 and 1999 Blue Poppy Press, USA.
This UK revised edition ©2000 W. Foulsham & Co. Ltd.

Neither the editors of W. Foulsham and Co. Ltd nor the author
nor the copyright holder nor the publisher take responsibility for
any possible consequences from any treatment, procedure, test,
exercise, action or application of medication or preparation by any
person reading or following the information in this book. The
publication of this book does not constitute the practice of medicine,
and this book does not attempt to replace your doctor. The author
and publisher advise the reader to check with a doctor before
administering any medication or undertaking any course of
treatment or exercise.

Typeset by Grafica, Bournemouth
Printed in Great Britain by St. Edmundsbury Press, Bury St. Edmunds, Suffolk.

CONTENTS

PREFACE

I have been practising traditional Chinese medicine in the United States of America for almost 20 years. During that time, I have mostly specialised in Chinese medical gynaecology, paediatrics and what Chinese doctors call internal medicine. Insomnia – called either *bu mian,* no sleep, or *shi mian,* loss of sleep in Chinese – has been one of Chinese medicine's core internal diseases for at least 2,000 years.

Although I have written numerous textbooks and clinical manuals for professionals on all aspects of Chinese medicine, up till now there has not been any simple discussion of the Chinese medical diagnosis and treatment of insomnia written specifically for the layperson. Therefore, I have created this book for sufferers of insomnia, their friends and families. Hopefully, the reader will find that traditional Chinese medicine is an enlightening and empowering alternative or complement to more conventional treatment. Chinese medicine has a whole and holistic, centuries-old, well-developed and coherent theory about the cause and treatment of insomnia. Not only is this theory enlightening – providing as it does an entirely different perspective on this common complaint from modern Western medicine – it is also empowering. Based on this theory, the reader will find there are all sorts of things, most of which are free or very low cost, which they can do for themselves in order to relieve and even cure their insomnia.

Insomnia does not have to occur. If it does, Chinese medicine has ways to cure or alleviate it.

Bob Flaws

INTRODUCTION

ocelyne was distraught. She had been tossing and turning in bed for hours. The clock by her bedside said it was 3 a.m., and tomorrow she had to give an important presentation. How was she ever going to be able to pull it off unless she fell asleep immediately? However, the more she fretted over not being able to sleep, the more tense and awake she became. What was worse, Jocelyne hadn't been able to get a good night's sleep in weeks. During the day, she was exhausted, but, when it came time to lie down at night, her mind would not turn off and her eyes would not close. It was getting so that she really dreaded the coming of bedtime and the special torture of sleeplessness it brought.

Sound familiar? If so, this book may very well help you break the cycle of insomnia. Practitioners of Traditional Chinese Medicine have been treating insomnia safely and effectively for tens of centuries.

This book is a layperson's guide to the diagnosis and treatment of insomnia with Chinese medicine. In it, you will learn what causes insomnia *and what you can do about it.* Hopefully, you will be able to identify yourself and your symptoms in these pages. If you can see yourself in the signs and symptoms I discuss below, I feel confident I will be able to share with you a number of self-help techniques which can minimise your discomfort. I have been a professional practitioner of Chinese medicine for almost 20 years, and I have helped scores of Western patients cure or relieve their insomnia. Chinese medicine cannot cure every disease, but when it comes to insomnia, Chinese medicine is the best alternative I know. When someone calls me and says that insomnia is their major complaint, I know that, if they follow my advice, together we can cure or at least improve their chances of getting a good night's sleep.

WHAT IS INSOMNIA?

According to *The Merck Manual*, the clinical Bible of Western doctors, insomnia refers to 'Difficulty in sleeping, or disturbed sleep patterns leaving the perception of insufficient sleep'.[1] Insomnia is a common symptom and may be due to a number of emotional and physical disorders.

TYPES OF INSOMNIA

Western medicine recognises at least three types of insomnia. The first is called initial insomnia. This refers to difficulty falling asleep after having lain down at night. The person cannot enter sleep at night. This is commonly associated with emotional disturbances, such as anxiety, a phobic state or depression. The second type of insomnia is called matitudinal insomnia or early morning wakening. The person is able to fall asleep, but then they wake up early in the morning, several hours before it is time to arise. Once awake, they then cannot fall back asleep. This pattern of early waking is a common phenomenon of ageing. However, even though it is common, it is nonetheless painful for its sufferers. In some cases, this type of insomnia may also be associated with depression. The third type of insomnia is called inverted sleep rhythm. If older patients with insomnia overuse sedative medications, they may be drowsy in the morning and doze all day. Then, when it comes time to sleep at night, they no longer feel tired. If the dose of sedatives is increased, the patient may feel restless, clouded, dazed or confused at night. If they suspend their sedative medication, their insomnia tends to return full force.

───────────────────────

[1] *The Merck Manual of Diagnosis and Therapy*, Robert Berkow, MD, editor, Merck, Sharp and Dohme Research Laboratories, Rahway, NJ, 1987, p. 1376

CAUSES OF INSOMNIA

Some people just sleep less than others. When insomnia is longstanding with little apparent relationship to immediate physical or psychological occurrences, this is called primary insomnia. If insomnia is due to pain, anxiety or depression, this is called secondary insomnia. In other words, the insomnia is secondary to another factor in the person's life. When insomnia is of relatively recent onset, it is usually due to current anxieties, such as relationship issues, problems at work, financial troubles or concern over one's health. However, as we will see below, insomnia may follow a prolonged or extreme febrile (i.e., feverish) disease and may occur in women around the menses, after giving birth, or around or after menopause, due to physical events associated with female physiology.

HOW WESTERN MEDICINE
TREATS INSOMNIA

When Western doctors try to treat insomnia, they usually do so using a combination of advice coupled with a prescription for one or more Western pharmaceuticals. The advice given might include suggestions such as getting more exercise, trying to relax or drinking warm milk before bed. As we will see below, the Chinese Medicine Practitioner may also give similar advice but on an individual basis. For some patients, getting more exercise may be beneficial, while for others it might aggravate their insomnia. Likewise, warm milk may help certain people sleep but worsen others' restlessness at night. A practitioner of Chinese medicine gives very specific advice to each individual patient.

With regards to Western medication, nowadays hypnotic drugs such as Zoplicone and Zolpidan are more frequently prescribed for insomnia as they are considered to be less addictive than some and have less of a hangover after-effect.

Benzodiazepines are also prescribed. They tend to be for short-term insomnia related to emotional upset. Examples of these drugs include Nitrazepan, Temazepan and Diazepan or Valium. Valium or Diazepan is the least frequently used these days as it is not as long lasting as the other medications. Antihistamines may also be taken due to their sedating effect.

Most GPs try to find the cause of the insomnia prior to prescribing medication. If the insomnia is chronic or long term they try to avoid using medication due to the highly addictive nature of the drugs. All hypnotics or sedatives may be addictive, involve a risk of overdose and when discontinued produce withdrawal symptoms which can include the recurrence of insomnia. Furthermore, because they are sedatives, it is important that persons taking these types of medication take care when engaging in any activity which requires mental alertness, judgement, or physical coordination, such as driving.

Some of the common adverse side-effects of sedatives and hypnotics are drowsiness, lethargy and 'hangover'. Less often, there can also be hives, nausea and vomiting. Ironically, in older patients, any sedative may cause restlessness and over-excitement. It is also sad but true that many patients take higher doses than they should or will admit to, thus causing slurring of speech, lack of coordination and shaking due to overdose. Sedatives are basically addictive in the same way that alcohol, opiates, antihistamines and antidepressants are. It is not surprising that a lot of people are reluctant to take sedatives.

Chinese medicine, on the other hand, has a number of safe, effective, low-cost and non-addictive alternatives which have been used in Asia for hundreds and thousands of years.

EAST IS EAST AND WEST IS WEST

In order for the reader to understand and make sense of the rest of this book on Chinese medicine and insomnia, one must understand that Chinese medicine is a distinct and separate system of medical thought and practice from modern Western medicine. This means that one must shift models of reality when it comes to thinking about Chinese medicine. It has taken the Chinese more than 2,000 years to develop this medical system. In fact, Chinese medicine is the oldest continually practised, literate, professional medicine in the world. As such one cannot understand Chinese medicine by trying to explain it in Western scientific or medical terms.

Many people reading this book may have studied biology at school or college. Whether we recognise it or not, most of us Westerners think of what we learned about the human body at school as 'the really real' description of reality, not one possible description. However, if Chinese medicine is to make any sense to Westerners at all, one must be able to entertain the notion that there are potentially other valid descriptions of the human body, its functions, health and disease. In grappling with this fundamentally important issue, it is useful to think about the concepts of a map and the terrain it describes.

If we take the United States of America as an example, we can have numerous different maps of its land mass. One map might show population. Another might show per capita incomes. Another might show religious or ethnic distributions. Yet another might be a road map. And still another might be a map showing political, i.e., state boundaries. In fact, there could be an infinite number of potentially different maps of the United States depending on what one was trying to show and do. As long as the map is based on accurate information and has been created with self-consistent logic, one map is not necessarily more correct than another. The issue is to use the right map for what you are trying to do. If one wants to drive from Chicago to Washington DC, then a road map may be the right one *for that job* but is not necessarily a truer or 'more real' description of the United States than a map showing annual rainfall.

What I am getting at here is that *the map is not the terrain.* The Western biological map of the human body is only one potentially useful medical map. It is no more true than the traditional Chinese medical map, and the 'facts' of one map cannot be reduced to the criteria or standards of another *unless they share the same logic right from the beginning*. As long as the Western medical map is capable of solving a person's disease in a cost-effective, time-efficient manner without side effects or iatrogenesis (meaning doctor-caused disease), then it is a useful map. Chinese medicine needs to be judged in the same way. The Chinese medical map of health and disease is just as 'real' as the Western biological map as long as, by using it, professional practitioners are able to solve their patients' health problems in a safe and effective way.

The following chapter is an introduction to some of the fundamental concepts of Chinese medicine. If you have a basic understanding of some of these fundamental concepts you will be able to appreciate how Chinese medicine may help in the treatment of insomnia.

AN OVERVIEW OF THE CHINESE MEDICAL MAP

In this chapter, we will look at an overview of Chinese medicine. In particular, we will discuss yin and yang, qi, blood and essence, the viscera and bowels, and the channels and network vessels. In the following chapter, we will go on to see how Chinese medicine views wakefulness and sleep. After that, we will look at the Chinese medical diagnosis and treatment of the various patterns of insomnia identified by Practitioners of Chinese Medicine. Should you find any of the language or terms used to describe the concepts of Chinese medicine difficult to understand, there is a glossary at the back of the book to which you can refer.

YIN AND YANG

To understand Chinese medicine, one must first understand the concepts of yin and yang since these are the most basic concepts in this system. Yin and yang are the cornerstones for understanding, diagnosing and treating the body and mind in Chinese medicine. In a sense, all the other theories and concepts of Chinese medicine are simply an elaboration of yin and yang. Most people have probably already heard of yin and yang but may not have a clear idea of what these terms mean.

The concepts of yin and yang can be used to describe everything that exists in the universe, including all the parts and functions of the body. Originally, yin referred to the shady side of a hill and yang to the sunny side of the hill. Since sunshine and shade are two interdependent sides of a single reality, these two aspects of the hill are seen as part of a single whole. Other examples of yin and yang are that night exists only in relation to day and cold exists only in relation to heat. According to

Chinese thought, every single thing that exists in the universe has these two aspects, a yin and a yang. Thus everything has a front and a back, a top and a bottom, a left and a right, and a beginning and an end. However, something is yin or yang *only in relation to its paired complement.* Nothing is in itself yin or yang.

It is the concepts of yin and yang that make Chinese medicine a holistic medicine. This is because, based on this unitary and complementary vision of reality, no body part or body function is viewed as separate or isolated from the whole person. The table below shows a partial list of yin and yang pairs as they apply to the body.

Yin	Yang
form	function
organs	bowels
blood	qi
inside	outside
front of body	back of body
right side	left side
lower body	upper body
cool, cold	warm, hot
stillness	activity, movement

It is vital to remember that each item listed is either yin or yang only in relation to its complementary partner. Nothing is absolutely or within itself either yin or yang. As we can see from the above list, it is possible to describe every aspect of the body in terms of yin and yang.

Qi

Qi (pronounced chee) and blood are the two most important complementary pairs of yin and yang within the human body. It is said that, in the world, yin and yang are water and fire, but in the human body, yin and yang are blood and qi. Qi is yang in relation to blood which is yin. Qi is often translated as energy and certainly energy is a manifestation of qi. Chinese language scholars would say, however, that qi is larger than any single type of energy described by modern Western science. Paul Unschuld, a well-known Sinologist, translates the word qi as influences. This conveys the sense that qi is what is responsible for change and movement. So, with regard to Chinese medicine, qi is that which motivates all movement and transformation or change.

In Chinese medicine, qi is defined as having five specific functions:

1. Defence
It is qi which is responsible for protecting the exterior of the body from invasion by external pathogens. This form of qi, called defensive qi, flows through the exterior or outer portion of the body.

2. Transformation
Qi transforms substances so that they can be utilised by the body. An example of this function is the transformation of the food we eat into nutrients to nourish the body, which then produces more qi and blood.

3. Warming
Qi, being relatively yang, is inherently warm and one of the main functions of the qi is to warm the entire body, both inside and out. If this warming function of the qi is weak, then the lack of warmth and resulting cold may cause the flow of qi and blood

to become congealed, in a similar way to the cold's effect on water – producing ice.

4. Restraint
It is qi which holds all the organs and substances in their proper place. Thus all the organs, blood and fluids need qi to keep them from falling or leaking out of their specific pathways. If this function of the qi is weak, then problems like uterine prolapse, easy bruising or urinary incontinence may occur.

5. Transportation
Qi provides the motivating force for all transportation and movement in the body. Every aspect of the body that moves is moved by the qi. The qi moves the blood and body fluids throughout the body. It moves food through the stomach and blood through the vessels.

BLOOD

In Chinese medicine, blood refers to the red fluid that flows through our vessels the same as in modern Western medicine, but it also has meanings and implications that are different from those in modern Western medicine. Most basically, blood is the substance that nourishes and moistens all the body tissues. Without blood, body tissues cannot function properly. Additionally, when there is insufficient blood or it is scanty, tissues become dry and wither.

Qi and blood are closely interrelated. It is said that, 'Qi is the commander of the blood and blood is the mother of qi.' This means that it is qi which moves the blood but that it is the blood which provides the nourishment and physical foundation for the creation and existence of the qi.

In Chinese medicine, blood provides the following functions for the body:

1. Nourishment

Blood nourishes the body. Along with qi, the blood goes to every part of the body. If the blood is insufficient, function decreases and tissues atrophy or shrink.

2. Moistening

Blood moistens the body tissues. This includes the skin, eyes and ligaments and tendons or what are simply called the sinews in Chinese medicine. Thus blood insufficiency can cause drying out and consequent stiffening of various tissues throughout the body.

3. Blood provides the material foundation for the spirit or mind

In Chinese medicine, the spirit, mind and body are considered as one. The spirit is a great accumulation of qi. The blood (yin) supplies the material support and nourishment for the spirit/mind (yang), allowing it to become 'bright' (i.e., conscious and clever), and stay rooted in the body. If blood is insufficient, the spirit/mind can 'float', causing problems such as insomnia, agitation and unrest.

ESSENCE

Along with qi and blood, essence is one of the three most important constituents of the body. Essence is the most fundamental, essential material the body utilises for its growth, maturation and reproduction. There are two forms of this essence. We inherit essence from our parents and we also produce our own essence from the food and drink which we consume and the air we breathe.

The essence which comes from our parents is what determines our basic constitution, strength and vitality. We each have a finite, limited amount of this inherited essence. It is important to protect and conserve this essence because all bodily functions depend upon it and, when it is gone, we die. Thus the depletion of essence has serious implications for our overall health and well-being. Happily, the essence derived from food and drink helps to bolster and support this inherited essence. So, if we eat well and do not consume more qi and blood than we create each day, then when we sleep at night, this surplus qi and more especially blood is transformed into essence.

THE VISCERA AND BOWELS

In Chinese medicine, the internal organs (called viscera so as not to become confused with the Western biological entities of the same name) have a much wider area of function and influence than in Western medicine. Each viscus has very distinct responsibilities for maintaining the physical and psychological health of the individual. When thinking about the internal viscera according to Chinese medicine, it is more accurate to view them as spheres of influence or a network that spreads throughout the body, rather than as a distinct and separate physical organ as described by Western science. This is why the famous German Sinologist, Manfred Porkert, refers to them as orbs rather than as organs. In Chinese medicine, the relationship between the various viscera and other parts of the body is made possible by the channel and network vessel system which we will discuss below.

In Chinese medicine, there are five main viscera which are relatively yin and six main bowels which are relatively yang. The five yin viscera are the heart, lungs, liver, spleen and kidneys. The six yang bowels are the stomach, small intestine, large intestine, gallbladder, urinary bladder and a system that Chinese medicine refers to as the triple burner. All the functions of the entire body are subsumed or described under these eleven organs or spheres of influence. Chinese medicine as a system does not have a pancreas, a pituitary gland or the ovaries as their functions and others are described by the sphere of influence of the five viscera and six bowels.

Within this system, the five viscera are the most important. These are the organs that Chinese medicine says are responsible for the creation and transformation of qi and blood and the storage of essence. For instance, the kidneys are responsible for the excretion of urine, but in addition they are responsible for hearing, the strength of the bones, sex, reproduction, maturation and growth, the lower and upper back, and the lower legs in general and the knees in particular.

VISCERAL CORRESPONDENCES

Organ	Tissue	Sense	Spirit	Emotion
Kidneys	bones/head hair	hearing	will	fear
Liver	sinews	sight	ethereal soul	anger
Spleen	flesh	taste	thought	thinking/worry
Lungs	skin/body hair	smell	corporeal soul	grief/sadness
Heart	blood vessels	speech	spirit	joy/fright

The Chinese viscera may have the same names and even some overlapping functions but they are quite different from the organs of modern Western medicine. Each of the five Chinese medical viscera also has a corresponding tissue, sense, spirit and emotion related to it. These are outlined in the table above.

In addition, each Chinese medical viscus or bowel possesses both a yin and a yang aspect. The yin aspect of a viscus or bowel refers to its substantial nature or tangible form. An organ's yin is responsible for the nurturing, cooling and moistening of that viscus or bowel. The yang aspect of the viscus or bowel represents its functional activities or what it does. An organ's yang aspect is also warming. These two aspects, yin and yang, form and function, cooling and heating, when balanced create good health. If either yin or yang becomes too strong or too weak, the result will be disease.

THE KIDNEYS

In Chinese medicine, the kidneys are considered to be the foundation of our life. Since the developing foetus is shaped like a kidney and because the kidneys are the main viscus for the storage of inherited essence, the kidneys are referred to as the prenatal root. Thus, keeping the kidney qi strong and kidney yin and yang in relative balance is considered essential to good health and longevity. From a Chinese medical point of view the kidneys have certain specific functions:

1. The kidneys are considered responsible for human reproduction, development and maturation
These are the same functions we used when describing the essence. This is because the essence is stored in the kidneys. Health problems related to reproduction, development and maturation are considered to be problems of the kidney essence. Excessive sexual activity, drug use, or simple prolonged over-exhaustion can all damage and consume kidney essence. Kidney essence is also consumed by the simple act of ageing.

2. The kidneys are the foundation of water metabolism
The kidneys work in coordination with the lungs and spleen to ensure that water is spread properly throughout the body and

that excess water is excreted as urination. Therefore, problems such as oedema, excessive dryness or excessive day-time or night-time urination can indicate a weakness of kidney function.

3. The kidneys are responsible for hearing since the kidneys open through the portals of the ears

Therefore, auditory problems such as diminished hearing and ringing in the ears can be due to kidney weakness.

4. The kidneys rule the grasping of qi

This means that one of the functions of the kidney qi is to pull down or absorb the breath from the lungs and root it in the lower abdomen. Certain types of asthma and chronic cough are the result of a weakness in this kidney function.

5. The kidneys rule the bones and marrow

This means that problems of the bones, such as osteoporosis, degenerative disc disease and weak legs and knees can all reflect a kidney problem.

6. Kidney yin and yang are the foundation for the yin and yang of all the other organs and bowels and body tissues of the entire body

This is another way of saying that the kidneys are the foundation of our life. If either kidney yin or yang is insufficient, eventually the yin or yang of the other organs will also become insufficient. The clinical implications of this will become more clear when we look at the various case histories involving low back pain.

7. The kidneys store the will

If kidney qi is insufficient, this aspect of our human nature can be weakened. Conversely, pushing ourselves to extremes, such as long-distance running or cycling, can eventually exhaust our kidneys.

8. Fear is the emotion associated with the kidneys
This means that fear can manifest when the kidney qi is insufficient. Vice versa, constant or excessive fear can damage the kidneys and make them weak.

9. The low back is the mansion of the kidneys
This means that, of all the areas of the body, the low back is the most closely related to the health of the kidneys. If the kidneys are weak, then there may be low back pain. It is because of this and the fact that the kidneys are associated with the bones that the kidneys are the first and most important viscus in terms of the health and well-being of the low back according to Chinese medicine.

THE LIVER

In Chinese medicine, the liver is associated with one's emotional state, with digestion and with menstruation in women. Specifically the functions of the Chinese medical concept of the liver include:

1. The liver controls coursing and discharge
Coursing and discharge refer to the uninhibited spreading of qi to every part of the body. If the liver is not able to maintain the free and smooth flow of qi throughout the body, multiple physical and emotional symptoms can develop. This function of the liver is most easily damaged by emotional causes and, in particular, by anger and frustration. For example, if the liver is stressed due to pent-up anger, the flow of liver qi can become depressed or stagnate.

Liver qi stagnation can cause a wide range of health problems, including PMS, chronic digestive disturbance, depression and insomnia. Therefore, it is essential to keep our liver qi flowing freely.

2. The liver stores the blood

This means that the liver regulates the amount of blood in circulation. In particular, when the body is at rest, the blood in the extremities returns to the liver. As an extension of this, it is said in Chinese medicine that the liver is yin in form but yang in function. Thus the liver requires sufficient blood to keep it and its associated tissues moist and supple, cool and relaxed.

3. The liver controls the sinews

The sinews refer mainly to the tendons and ligaments in the body. Proper function of the tendons and ligaments depends upon the nourishment of liver blood to keep them moist and supple.

4. The liver opens into the portals of the eyes

The eyes are the specific sense organ corresponding to the liver. Therefore, many eye problems are related to the liver in Chinese medicine.

5. The emotion associated with the liver is anger

Anger is the emotion that typically arises when the liver is diseased, especially when its qi does not flow freely. Conversely, anger damages the liver. Thus the emotions related to the stagnation of qi in the liver are frustration, anger and rage.

THE HEART

Although the heart is the emperor of the body-mind according to Chinese medicine, it does not play as large a role in the creation and treatment of disease as one might think. Rather than the emperor initiating the cause of disease, in Chinese medicine, mostly enduring disease eventually affects the heart. Especially in terms of insomnia, disturbances of the heart tend to be secondary rather than primary. By this I mean that first some other viscus or bowel becomes diseased and then the heart feels the negative effect. The Chinese medical concept of the heart has the following specific functions:

1. The heart governs the blood
This means that it is the heart qi which 'stirs' or moves the blood within its vessels. This is roughly analogous to the heart's pumping the blood in Western medicine. The pulsation of the blood through the arteries due to the contraction of the heart is referred to as the 'stirring of the pulse'. In fact, the Chinese word for pulse and vessel is the same. So this could also be translated as the 'stirring of the vessels'.

2. The heart stores the spirit
The spirit refers to the mind in Chinese medicine. Therefore, this statement underscores that mental function, mental clarity and mental equilibrium are all associated with the heart. If the heart does not receive enough qi or blood or if the heart is disturbed by something, the spirit may become restless and this may produce symptoms of mental-emotional unrest, such as heart palpitations, insomnia and profuse dreams.

3. The heart governs the vessels
This statement is very close to number 1 above. The vessels refer to the blood vessels and also to the pulse.

4. The heart governs speech
If heart function becomes abnormal, this may be reflected in various speech problems such as stuttering or raving and delirious speech, muttering to oneself and speaking incoherently.

5. The heart opens into the portal of the tongue
The heart has a special relationship with the tongue, especially its tip. Heart problems may manifest as sores on the tip of the tongue.

6. Joy is the emotion associated with the heart
The emotion of joy helps ease the flow of qi (and therefore blood). It helps us to relax and we feel more harmonious. The emotion of joy is very healing, as is laughter. Joy and laughter are associated with the heart. If there is too much joy, such as when someone becomes overly excited, this can be damaging to the heart. It is interesting to look at manic depression in terms of these polar opposites: on the one hand the person is flat, emotionless and depressed whilst on the other they are manic and wildly excited. It is also interesting that many famous comedians die of heart attacks or suffer from depression.

THE SPLEEN

The role of the spleen in Chinese medicine is very wide-reaching and more important then in Western medicine. This is an excellent illustration of how these two systems of medicine differ in their view of the internal organs and their functions. In Chinese medicine, the spleen plays a pivotal role in the creation of qi and blood and in the circulation and transformation of body fluids. The main functions of the spleen relating to insomnia are:

1. The spleen governs movement and transformation
This refers to the movement and transformation of foods and liquids through the digestive system. In this case, movement and transformation may be considered to be digestion. Movement and transformation may also refer to the movement and transformation of body fluids through the body. It is the spleen qi which is largely responsible for controlling liquid metabolism in the body.

2. The spleen restrains the blood

As mentioned above, one of the five functions of the qi is to restrain the fluids of the body, including the blood, within their proper channels and reservoirs. If the spleen qi is healthy and abundant, then the blood is held within its vessels properly. Conversely, if the spleen qi becomes weak and insufficient, then the blood may flow outside its channels and vessels resulting in various types of pathological bleeding. This includes various types of pathological bleeding associated with the menstrual cycle.

3. The spleen stores the constructive

The constructive is one of the types of qi in the body. Specifically, it is the qi that is responsible for nourishing and constructing the body and its tissues. This constructive qi is closely associated with the process of digestion and the creation of qi and blood out of food and liquids. If the spleen fails to store or runs out of constructive qi, then the person first becomes hungry, and eventually becomes fatigued.

4. The spleen governs the muscles and flesh

This statement is closely allied to the previous one. It is the constructive qi which constructs or nourishes the muscles and flesh. If there is sufficient spleen qi producing sufficient constructive qi, then the person's body is well fleshed and rounded. In addition, their muscles are normally strong. Conversely, if the spleen becomes weak, this may lead to emaciation and/or lack of strength.

5. The spleen governs the four limbs

This means that the strength and function of the four limbs is closely associated with the spleen. If the spleen is healthy and strong, then there is sufficient strength in the four limbs and warmth in the four extremities. If the spleen becomes weak and insufficient, then there may be lack of strength in the four limbs, lack of warmth in the extremities or even tingling and numbness in the extremities.

6. The spleen opens into the portal of the mouth
Just as the ears are the portals of the kidneys, the eyes are the portals of the liver, and the tongue is the portal of the heart, the mouth is the portal of the spleen. Therefore, spleen disease often manifests as sores on the mouth or lips or bleeding from the gums.

7. Thought is the emotion associated with the spleen
In the West, we do not usually think of thought as an emotion per se. Be that as it may, in Chinese medicine it is classified along with anger, joy, fear, grief and melancholy. In particular, thinking, or perhaps I should say overthinking or obsessive thinking, causes the spleen qi to 'bind'. This means that the spleen qi does not flow harmoniously and this typically manifests as loss of appetite, abdominal bloating after meals and indigestion.

8. The spleen is the source of engenderment and transformation
Engenderment and transformation refer to the creation or production of the qi and blood out of the food and drink we take in each day. If the spleen receives adequate food and drink and then properly transforms that food and drink, it engenders or creates the qi and blood. Although the kidneys and lungs also participate in the creation of the qi, while the kidneys and heart also participate in the creation of the blood, the spleen is the pivotal viscus in both processes. Spleen qi weakness and insufficiency is one of the main causes of qi and blood deficiency and weakness.

THE LUNGS

The lungs are, perhaps, not as important in relation to insomnia as the other Chinese viscera. However, like the heart, the lungs often bear the brunt of disease processes initiated in other viscera and bowels. As in Western medicine, the lungs are often subject to externally invading pathogens resulting in respiratory tract diseases. However, the lungs' sphere of influence also includes the skin and fluid metabolism. The main functions of the lungs according to Chinese medicine are:

1. The lungs govern the qi
Specifically, the lungs govern the downward spread and circulation of the qi. It is the lung qi which moves all the rest of the qi in the body out to the edges and from the top of the body downwards. The lung qi is like a sprinkler spraying out qi. This downward qi then ensures body fluids are moved throughout the body, down to the kidneys and bladder and, eventually, out of the body.

2. The lungs govern the skin and hair
The skin and body hair correspond with the lungs. If the lungs become diseased, this often manifests as skin problems.

3. The lungs govern the voice
If there is sufficient lung qi, the voice is strong and clear. If there is insufficient lung qi, then the voice is weak and the person tries not to speak as a way of conserving their energy.

4. The lungs govern the free flow and regulation of the water passageways
This statement emphasises the lung qi's role in moving body fluids outwards and downwards throughout the body, to arrive ultimately at the urinary bladder. If the lung qi fails to maintain the free flow and regulation of the water passageways, then

fluids will collect and transform into dampness, thus producing water swelling or oedema.

5. The lungs govern the defensive exterior

We say above that the qi defends the body against invasion by external pathogens. In Chinese medicine, the exterior-most layer of the body is the area where the defensive qi circulates and is the place where this defence, therefore, takes place. In particular, it is the lungs which govern this defensive qi. If the lungs function normally and there is sufficient defensive qi, then the body cannot be invaded by external pathogens. If the lungs are weak and the defensive qi is insufficient, then external pathogens may easily invade the exterior of the body, causing complaints such as colds, flus and allergies.

6. The lungs are the florid canopy

This means that the lungs are like a tent spreading over the top of all the other viscera and bowels. On the one hand, they are the first viscus to be assaulted by external pathogens invading the body from the top. On the other, any pathogenic qi moving upwards in the body eventually may accumulate in and affect the lungs.

7. The lungs are the delicate viscus

Because the lungs are the most delicate of all the viscera and bowels, they are the most easily invaded by external pathogens. This is the Chinese explanation for the prevalence of colds and flus in comparison to other types of diseases.

8. The lungs form nasal mucus

If the lungs are functioning correctly, there should not be any runny nose or nasal congestion.

9. The lungs open into the portal of the nose

This statement is similar to the one above. However, it approaches the issue from a slightly different perspective. The implication of this statement is that diseases having to do with the nose and its function are often associated with the Chinese medical idea of the lungs.

Each yin viscus is paired with a yang bowel in a yin–yang or exterior–interior relationship. The kidneys are paired with the urinary bladder, the liver is paired with the gallbladder, the heart is paired with the small intestine, the spleen is paired with the stomach, and the lungs are paired with the large intestine. The yin viscus is relatively more interior and the yang bowel is relatively more exterior. In the case of the urinary bladder, gallbladder and stomach, these bowels receive their qi from their paired viscus and function very much as an extension of that viscus. The relationship between the other two viscera and bowels is not as close.

In terms of insomnia, Chinese medical theory only concerns itself with two of the six bowels. These are the gallbladder and the stomach.

THE GALLBLADDER

The main functions of the gallbladder in terms of insomnia according to the principles of Chinese medicine are:

1. The gallbladder governs decision

In Chinese medicine, the liver is likened to a general who plans strategy for the body, while the gallbladder is likened to a judge. According to this point of view, if a person lacks gallbladder qi, they will have trouble making decisions. They may also be timid and hesitant. While courage in the West is associated with the heart (*coeur* = courage), bravery in the East is associated with the gallbladder. Actually, this is also an old Western idea as well. When someone is very forward and brazen, we say that 'They have gall'. Conversely, if someone is excessively timid, this may be due to gallbladder qi vacuity or insufficiency. In Chinese medicine, this is called 'gallbladder timidity'.

2. The liver and gallbladder have the same palace
This statement underscores the particularly close relationship between the liver and gallbladder.

3. If there is qi because of a robust gallbladder, evils are not able to enter
These two statements are very close to statements in Chinese medicine about the heart, saying that the heart is the sovereign of the body and that if spirit abides (in the heart), then evils cannot enter. Both these statements elevate the gallbladder to a place of importance in the body it does not hold in Western medicine and link the gallbladder in a way to the heart and its spirit.

THE STOMACH

There are a number of important functions which relate to the stomach in Chinese medicine due to the stomach's pivotal role in digestion and, therefore, in the creation of qi and blood. Below we will only discuss those functions which we will use later in our discussion of the disease causes and disease mechanisms of insomnia in Chinese medicine.

1. The stomach governs intake
This means that the stomach is the first to receive foods and drinks ingested into the body.

2. The stomach governs downbearing of the turbid
The process of digestion in Chinese medicine is likened to the process of fermentation and then distillation. The stomach is concerned with the process of fermentation whereby foods and

liquids are 'rotted and ripened'. This rotting and ripening allows for the separation of clear and turbid parts of the digestate. The spleen sends the clear parts upwards to the lungs and heart to become the qi and blood respectively. The stomach's job is to send the turbid part down to be excreted as waste from the large intestine and bladder.

3. Stomach heat may exploit the heart

If, for any reason, abnormal or pathological heat collects in the stomach, it may affect the heart. As heat is yang and has an innate tendency to move upwards and outwards, and as the heart is located above the stomach in Chinese medicine, heat in the stomach may exploit or harass the heart situated above it.

4. The stomach is the origin of the defensive qi

We have seen above that the defensive qi is the qi which defends the exterior of the body from invasion by external pathogens. This defensive qi's other job is to warm the internal organs. According to some points of view, the stomach is the origin of the defensive qi. This is because it is in the stomach that the clear and turbid parts of the digestate are separated, and the defensive qi is made out of a further refinement of the turbid part of this digestate. Therefore, the stomach has a definite relationship with the defensive qi, and, as we will see below, this relationship can help to explain at least one type of insomnia.

Above I mentioned that there are five viscera and six bowels. The sixth bowel is called the triple burner. It is said in Chinese that, 'The triple burner has a function but no form.' The name triple burner refers to the three main areas of the torso. The upper burner is the chest. The middle burner is the space from the bottom of the ribcage to the level of the navel. The lower burner is the lower abdomen below the navel. These three spaces are called burners because all of the functions and transformations of the viscera and bowels that they contain act as 'warm' transformations similar to food cooking in a pot on a

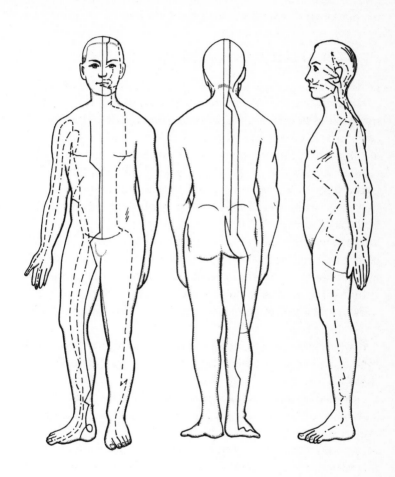

stove, or an alchemical transformation in a furnace. In fact, the triple burner is nothing other than a generalised concept of how the other viscera and bowels function together as an organic unit in terms of the digestion of foods and liquids and the circulation and transformation of body fluids.

THE CHANNELS AND NETWORK VESSELS

Each viscus and bowel has a corresponding channel with which it is connected. In Chinese medicine, the inside of the body is made up of the viscera and bowels. The outside of the body is composed of the sinews and bones, muscles and flesh, and skin and hair. It is the channels and network vessels (i.e., smaller connecting vessels) which connect the inside and the outside of the body. It is through these channels and network vessels that the viscera and bowels connect with their corresponding body tissues.

The channels and network vessel system is a unique feature of traditional Chinese medicine. These channels and vessels are different from the circulatory, nervous or lymphatic systems. The earliest reference to these channels and vessels is in *Nei Jing* (*The Inner Classic*), a text written around the 2nd or 3rd century BCE.

The channels and vessels perform two basic functions. They are the pathways by which the qi and blood circulate through the body and between the organs and tissues. Additionally, as mentioned above, the channels connect the viscera and bowels internally with the exterior part of the body. This channel and vessel system functions in the body much like an information or communication network. The channels allow the various parts of our body to cooperate and interact to maintain our lives.

This channel and network vessel system is complex. There are 12 primary channels, 6 yin and 6 yang, each with a specific pathway through the external body and connected with an internal organ (see diagrams on page 33). There are also extraordinary vessels, sinew channels, channel divergences, main network vessels, and ultimately countless finer and finer network vessels permeating the entire body. All of these form a closed loop or circuit similar to but distinct from the Western circulatory system.

Acupuncture points are places located on the major channels where there is a special concentration of qi and blood. As there is relatively more qi and blood accumulated at these points, the sites act as switches which can potentially influence the flow of qi and blood in the relevant channel. By stimulating these points in any of a number of different ways, one can speed up or slow down, make more or reduce, warm or cool down the qi and blood flowing in the channels and vessels. The main method of stimulating these points and thus adjusting the flow of qi and blood in the channels and vessels is to needle them and to heat them by moxibustion.[2] Other commonly used ways of stimulating these points and thus adjusting the qi and blood flowing through the channels and vessels are massage, cupping, the application of magnets, and the application of various herbal medicinals. If the channels and vessels are the pathways over which the qi and blood flow, then the acupuncture points are specific places where this flow can be influenced.

---

[2] Moxibustion refers to adding heat to an acupuncture point or area of the body by burning a dried herb, Folium Artemisae Argyii (*Ai Ye*), Oriental Mugwort, on, over or near the area to be warmed.

SLEEP AND WAKEFULNESS
IN CHINESE MEDICINE

Sleep and wakefulness are a yin–yang pair in Chinese medicine. Consciousness is called *shen ming* in Chinese medicine. *Shen* means the spirit, while *ming* means brightness or brilliance. In addition, the spirit is considered to be an accumulation of yang qi in the heart. In the closing to his monumental *Pi Wei Lun* (*Treatise on the Spleen and Stomach*), Li Dong-yuan, one of the four great masters of medicine of the Jin-Yuan dynasties (1280–1368 CE), explained the relationship between the spirit, qi and essence thus:

> Qi is the forefather of spirit and essence is the child of qi.
> (Therefore,) qi is the root of essence and spirit. Great is qi!

When yang qi ascends to the upper body to accumulate in the heart as spirit and to the sensory orifices of the head as clear yang qi, the mind is awake and the senses are conscious. The eyes and ears are open and functioning and the person is 'conscious of human affairs'.

Clear yang qi is produced out of the food and drink we take in each day as well as the air we breathe. It is the clear part of food and drink sent up to the lungs by the spleen that combines with the heavenly or great qi breathed in by the lungs that becomes the constructive qi which empowers, nourishes and constructs the body.

Sleep, on the other hand, is the sinking of this clear yang qi back downwards and into the core of the body to be 'enfolded' and nurtured by yin. The yang qi sinks back downwards and into the core of the body because it has been consumed by the day's activities. In other words, the processes of seeing, hearing, smelling, tasting, thinking, moving, emoting and all other life processes use up yang qi in the course of their activity. When we have used up a certain sufficiency of yang qi, we no longer have enough to keep our spirit bright and in contact with the outer world. During sleep, yin blood nourishes and transforms into yang qi. Thus when our yang qi has recuperated after a number of hours of sleep, we wake back up again, ready to face the challenges and activities of a new day.

The fact that our body's yang qi comes upwards and outwards around daybreak and retreats back downwards and inwards after the sun goes down is due to our body's qi being influenced by the larger qi of the external universe. The sun is called *tai yang* or supreme yang in Chinese. Its rising each morning is seen as a growth of yang qi in the world at large. At noon, this yang qi reaches its extreme and begins to descend and retreat again. Therefore, the ruling qi of day is yang, which grows from sun-up to noon and declines from noon to sundown, while the ruling qi of night is yin, which grows from sundown to midnight and declines from midnight to sun-up. Thus the body's yin and yang also follows suit. It is said in Chinese medicine, 'Humans exist within heaven and earth and, therefore, correspond (i.e., co-respond or resonate) with the sun and moon.'

The rate of consumption each day of our yang qi and the blood and yin which support and nourish it is dependent upon and proportional to each day's activities. When we are more active, we consume more yang qi. When we are less active, we consume less yang qi. So, on days when we work harder, we may feel more tired more quickly than on other days. Hence, we may want to go to sleep earlier and/or sleep longer. If, for some reason, we cannot go to sleep when we want to, we begin to consume even more qi (and blood) than usual. If we consume all the qi and blood that we manufactured that day, then we start dipping into our reserves. These reserves are the essence that is stored in each of the five viscera and whose major portion is stored in the kidneys. When push comes to shove or when the going gets tough, stored essence is tranformed into qi. From this point of view, essence is yin to qi's yang and yin essence may be transformed into yang qi.

If one has plenty of stored essence, then this is no big deal. The next day, if one eats and drinks properly and one's lungs are functioning correctly, and if one's activities do not use up all the qi and blood manufactured that day, then the surplus that is left over when we go to sleep the next night is converted back into stored essence.

AGE AND SLEEP

When we are babies, our viscera and bowels have not matured and our qi and blood are not plentiful and robust. Hence newborns need a lot of sleep. Their immature viscera and bowels do not produce enough qi and blood to keep their yang qi in the upper and outer part of their bodies for any length of time. As they grow their viscera and bowels mature. They become more and more efficient in transforming qi and blood out of the food they eat and the air they breathe.

As young adults, if a) we have a normal constitution, b) we are eating a relatively healthy diet, and c) we are not grossly overexerting ourselves every day, we make plenty more qi and blood each day than we consume. So, we make plenty of new essence to be stored in the five viscera and especially the kidneys. When we are young, we can overwork one day, and still be bright-eyed and bushy-tailed the next day. Or we are able to stay up all night in college and the next day be none the worse for wear.

Mostly, this superabundance of qi and blood and, subsequently, of acquired essence, is due to the spleen's maturation at around six years of age. It is said that the spleen is the postnatal root of qi and blood engenderment and transformation. This is because it is the spleen which is in charge of transforming or refining the pure or clear part of the digestate to become the qi and blood. Hence, the sufficiency of qi and blood and, consequently, acquired essence is primarily dependent upon a healthy spleen processing sufficient nutrition. If either the spleen is not given the raw materials to transform or the spleen qi is not capable of doing its duty, qi and blood production will not be up to par.

It is said in the *Nei Jing* (*The Inner Classic*), the so-called Bible of Chinese medicine written some 2,200 years ago, that the digestion begins to decline at around 35 years of age. Hence, the spleen does not make as much blood, and because there is not as much blood to nourish and moisten the skin, one begins to get wrinkles on the face. This clearly underscores that the ageing process begins with the decline of the process of digestion and the manufacture of qi and blood, and this process of digestion is governed and primarily based on the Chinese medical concept of the spleen.

This is also the explanation why we typically need more sleep and tire more easily after 35 years of age. We may look at our younger sisters and brothers in the full bloom of their 20s, carousing all night and getting up for work the next morning, and wonder how they do it. They do it because their spleens are still manufacturing so much qi and blood every day. However, past 35, we no longer make the same superabundance of qi and blood, and start drawing down on the yin essence stored in our kidneys.

This indicates that the ageing process in humans is concerned with the consumption of yin by yang. Yang is active and consumes yin, but, after a certain age, we no longer replace and replenish the yin we are using up. Hence, the ageing process is, at least in part, a process of drying up (since yin is cool and moist). Wrinkles, greying of the hair, poorer teeth, hair falling out and osteoporosis are all manifestations of the consumption and non-replacement of yin substance by yang function.

At first, decrease in qi and blood due to ageing may make us more easily fatigued and prompt us to go to bed earlier and sleep longer. Furthermore, a basic tenet of yin–yang theory is that yin checks or controls yang. If yin becomes so vacuous and weak that it cannot control yang, then yang may counterflow upwards and outwards. This upward and outward flow of yang is not a healthy movement. Yang is not rising upwards because there is a true superabundance of clear yang qi. Rather, it is rising up when it shouldn't because there is insufficient yin to hold it down. This explains why so many people develop matitudinal insomnia as they age. Yang qi runs out of steam at the end of the day and initially they go to sleep. But there is insufficient yin to enfold and hold yang down for long. Yang is relatively out of balance from yin, and so, as soon as the sun, *tai yang*, begins to move upwards in the world outside, our own yang also pops back up out of control too early in the morning.

This means that anything which stirs yang qi to move upwards and outwards may cause or aggravate insomnia, and we will look at some of the specific causes of this below. Some readers may, at this point, be thinking that, since consumption of yin is an inevitable part of ageing, that, past a certain age, there is nothing that can be done about insomnia. However, as we see below, Chinese medicine has simple, safe and effective ways of stimulating the body to produce more blood and yin, *thus counteracting the effects of the ageing process.*

THE UTERUS AND SLEEP

To the uninitiated, the above heading must seem very strange. What does the uterus have to do with sleep? In Chinese medicine, it is said that men and women are essentially the same *except that women have a uterus.* Since they have a uterus, they menstruate, can have babies, and lactate. According to Chinese medicine, this makes women more prone to insomnia, at least at certain times, than men are.

Menstruation is a discharge or loss of blood each month, and blood is part of yin. In fact, the famous Qing dynasty

(1644–1911 CE) Chinese gynaecologist, Fu Qing-zhu, said that the menstrual blood in women should not just be seen as blood but as the physical expression of their yin essence. When a woman is young and in good health, she is able to make a superabundance of blood each month, and this is discharged as the menses. Since she is making so much qi and blood because of her strong, healthy spleen, this blood loss causes no problem. However, in women with weak spleens or in many women as they age, they may experience insomnia each month either before, during or just after their period. If a woman's blood is scanty or deficient, when it is sent down by the heart to accumulate in the uterus in the pre-menstruum, she may not have enough yin blood left over to control yang qi. This yang qi counterflows upwards and outwards, manifesting as insomnia or wakefulness. Alternatively she may have enough blood for yin to control yang during the pre-menstruum, but not enough blood to control yang once she actually starts to lose blood with the menstrual flow. In this case, the woman may develop insomnia during or after her menses when it is said her blood is relatively empty.

Likewise, some women develop insomnia either during pregnancy or after delivery. In Chinese medicine, the baby's body is made out of the mother's essence and blood. Towards the end of the pregnancy when the baby has grown, some women will have used up so much blood and essence that their yin can no longer control their yang. In other cases, some women will lose so much blood and sweat during labour or with their postpartum lochia or vaginal discharge that now their yin is insufficient to control yang. Additionally, since breast milk is made out of the mother's blood according to Chinese medicine, women whose blood and yin are scanty to begin with often experience worsening of this yin vacuity during breast-feeding. This is why some women may develop insomnia associated with breast-feeding.

Finally, women in particular are prone to insomnia around the time of menopause. The pause in menstruation occurs because the body in its wisdom recognises that it can no longer support in a healthy manner either a monthly loss of blood during menstruation or another pregnancy. From the mid-30s onwards, some women will notice their menses becoming progressively less voluminous. This goes along with a decrease in blood production in turn due to a decrease in spleen function associated with ageing. As the woman gets into her 40s, she is not making sufficient blood to afford a monthly menstruation. This monthly loss of blood in many women actually causes a yin insufficiency and a relative yang excess or repletion. This is why many women develop insomnia around the time of menopause. It is due to the relationship of blood and essence and essence and yin. Hence, in Chinese medicine, we recognise that women, due to 'having a uterus', are at special risk for suffering from insomnia, either at certain times of the month or at certain times of their lives.

THE CHINESE MECHANISMS OF INSOMNIA

ow that we have explained some of the fundamental concepts of Chinese medicine and discussed sleep and wakefulness we can start to look more specifically at some of the mechanisms of imbalance which relate to insomnia in Chinese medicine.

DISEASE CAUSES AND MECHANISMS

According to Traditional Chinese Medicine, commonly known as TCM, there are at least eight basic causes and mechanisms of insomnia. TCM is a style or method of practising Chinese medicine which is widely used in both the West and modern China. It is the style that I use in my clinical practice. Common to each of the disease causes and mechanisms involved in insomnia is an underlying imbalance between yin and yang. Yin fails to control yang. The yang which is now out of control flows upwards and outwards as it is no longer held in check by the yin.

Heart–spleen dual vacuity

Heart–spleen dual vacuity may also be called heart–blood–spleen qi vacuity. If thinking, worry, overtaxation or fatigue are excessive, any of these may damage the spleen. Since the spleen is the root of qi and blood engenderment and transformation, spleen qi which is vacuous and weak will fail to manufacture and send up enough blood to the heart spirit. Spirit is nothing other than an accumulation of yang qi. If the heart does not receive sufficient blood to nourish and control this spirit, the heart spirit will grow restless and lose its tranquillity. Hence it cannot subside and be enfolded by and in yin at night. In Chinese medicine, the day is yang compared to the night being yin. So, during the day, yang qi is pre-eminent in the body, while at night, yin blood is pre-eminent within the human organism. Assuming the role of the blood is pre-eminent at night, if yin blood is insufficient and scanty, it tends to manifest this all the more strongly at night. As one ancient Chinese medical text puts it, 'If thinking and worry damage the spleen and spleen blood becomes debilitated and suffers detriment, insomnia may continue for years.'

It is interesting to note that thinking here simply means the process of thinking itself. Its ill effect does not depend on whether one's thoughts are good or bad. Thinking is a yang activity of the spirit which consumes yin blood. If thinking is excessive, then there will be excessive consumption of yin blood.

Although Chinese medical texts tend to emphasise the negative role of overthinking and too much work, too little exercise and an incorrect diet may also contribute to a heart–spleen vacuity. While too much work or exercise overly consumes the qi and blood manufactured by the spleen, too little exercise causes the qi mechanism to become stagnant. The qi mechanism is the mechanism of bearing up the pure or clear part of the digestate and bearing down the turbid part. This bearing up and down is dependent on the free and active flow of qi. If you fail to get sufficient exercise, the qi does not flow smoothly and freely, and the process of digestion and the subsequent creation and transformation of qi and blood is also sluggish and insufficient.

In addition, eating the wrong foods may also damage the spleen, thus resulting in a heart–blood vacuity. As we will see below, the process of digestion is a warm transformation of yang qi working on and refining yin substance. Therefore, eating too many chilled and uncooked foods and drinking iced liquids can douse the digestive fire of the spleen. Likewise, eating too many sugars and sweets may also damage the spleen. This includes too many sweet and juicy fruits and fruit juices, like oranges and peaches. Finally, eating too many dairy products and fatty foods may damage the spleen, leading to spleen vacuity or emptiness and consequent qi and blood vacuity.

Liver depression qi stagnation

As we have seen above, the liver's main job is to govern the coursing and discharge of all the qi in the body. This means that it is the liver's job to ensure that the flow of qi is smooth and freely flowing. If someone suffers from emotional stress and frustration, other qi is affected and cannot 'spread freely'. This frustration in turn affects the liver's coursing and discharging of the qi. Proportional to the frustration, the liver's coursing and discharging of the qi will become depressed and the qi flow stagnant. This is called liver depression qi stagnation. It is mostly due to stress and frustration or a thwarting of one's desires. Because none of us can fulfil all our wishes at the very moment we desire them, most adults suffer from some element of liver depression qi stagnation – the more stress and frustration, the more liver depression and qi stagnation.

In actual fact, liver depression qi stagnation due to emotional stress and frustration does not cause insomnia all by itself. However, if the liver becomes depressed, this typically leads to the spleen becoming vacuous and weak. This is because the liver 'controls' the spleen according to an ancient Chinese theory called five phase theory. Based on this theory, the spleen is usually the first viscus subsequently to become diseased after the liver becomes depressed. If the spleen becomes vacuous and weak, it will not engender and transform the qi and blood properly, and this then may lead to a heart–blood–spleen qi dual vacuity. In that case, heart blood is too vacuous to nourish and quiet the spirit. The spirit, which is nothing other than an accumulation of yang qi, becomes hyperactive or restless, and this restlessness manifests as wakefulness.

It is also possible for liver depression qi stagnation to lead to yin vacuity. The qi is what moves yin blood to nourish all the viscera and bowels of the body. As it is said in Chinese medicine:

> If the qi moves, the blood moves. If the qi stops, the blood stops.

If the qi does not flow freely, the blood and yin cannot flow freely to nourish the viscera and bowels. So, long-term or persistent liver depression qi stagnation eventually results in concomitant yin vacuity. In this case, yin fails to control yang which flushes upwards and outwards causing wakefulness. Since yin tends to become vacuous after the age of 35 or 40 in any case, the negative effects of liver depression depriving the viscera of sufficient nourishment by the blood and yin tend to become more apparent after this age. In Chinese medicine it is said, 'Yin is half consumed by 40 years of age.'

Liver depression transforming heat

There is a theory in Chinese medicine called The Theory of Similar Transformation. Since the body's living qi is yang, and therefore warm in nature, if anything causes this qi to back up and accumulate, it may cause such depressed and stagnant yang qi to transform into or manifest as pathological heat. So, it is said in Chinese medicine that persistent liver depression due to emotional stress and frustration may transform into heat or fire. This is called transformative or depressive heat. This transformation may also take place in a shorter period of time if frustration, stress and emotional upset are severe. It is said in Chinese medicine that, 'Any of the seven emotions may transform into fire if extreme.'

Fire is by nature yang and, therefore, tends to move upwards and outwards in the body, drafting along with it the body's host yang qi. In addition, this fire tends to collect in the upper part of the body and the heart. This pathological heat accumulating in the heart causes the spirit to flit around restlessly. Could you fall asleep if your house were on fire?

This tendency of depressive heat due to frustration and stress or anger and emotional upset to rise up and accumulate in the heart can be aggravated by eating hot, acrid, peppery foods. This includes chillies and peppers, but also greasy, fried, fatty foods, and alcohol. Overeating any of these can give rise to stomach heat which flares upwards to accumulate in the heart.

Since heat or fire is yang, it not only moves upwards and outwards in the body but also evaporates and consumes blood and yin. As we age, because yin is already being consumed, there is, therefore, a tendency for depression to transform into heat even more easily.

Yin vacuity, fire effulgence

If, for any reason, yin becomes truly vacuous and insufficient, yang may in turn become hyperactive. If yang becomes very hyperactive, it is called internal fire. Since yin is primarily associated with the kidneys and hyperactive yang is primarily associated with the liver, this is also referred to as kidney yin vacuity with ascendant hyperactivity of liver yang or liver yang harassing and stirring above. Such a kidney yin vacuity may be due to constitutional insufficiency, meaning that the person was simply not born with much yin to begin with. People with very thin bodies tend to suffer from constitutional yin vacuity. Such yin vacuity can be due to ageing as we have already seen or may also be due to long-term or severe disease and especially a febrile or feverish disease. In the latter, the pathological heat associated with the disease consumes and wastes the body's yin blood. Tuberculosis, or what is still called vacuity consumption in Chinese medicine, is a good example of this mechanism.

It is also possible for yin vacuity to be due to simply too much stirring or activity. In Chinese, the word *dong* means to stir. In the Jin-Yuan dynasties, Zhu Dan-xi, the last of the four great doctors of that era, said that, in human beings in general, 'Yang tends to be superabundant, while yin is typically insufficient' and that any activity may cause stirring of yang and further consumption of yin. By activity, Zhu meant any physical, mental or emotional activity. Zhu saw all of these activities as manifestations of stirring yang which consumes yin and leads to only more stirring of yang.

Zhu also singled out what, in Chinese, is referred to as 'bedroom taxation'. Simply put, this means too much sex, which can of course affect both men and women. Sexual desire in Chinese medicine is a pre-eminent manifestation of stirring yang. When we are filled with sexual desire, we say we are 'hot' with desire. We are all 'stirred up'. We are 'hot and bothered'. We might even need to take a cold shower to calm 'the flames of our desire'. All these colloquialisms point to the same truth that the Chinese have observed for centuries. In Chinese medicine, sexual desire and sexual activity are both a function of kidney fire or kidney yang. If there is excessive sexual desire which is unfulfilled, then this fire is stirred up and then depressed. This leads to liver depression transforming heat. Alternatively, if there is excessive sexual activity, this may lead to consumption and loss of yin. In both cases, too much desire or too much sex can lead to or worsen yin vacuity with its attendant loss of control over yang.

Anything which speeds up the body or pushes the body to prolonged excessive activity may lead to yin vacuity and yang hyperactivity. Things which speed up the body are caffeinated drinks, such as coffee, and recreational drugs, such as cocaine and amphetamines (or speed). Prolonged, excessive stirring refers to prolonged, excessive emotions or prolonged excessive activity, such as too much work or exercise. Any of these can waste yin and stir yang hyperactively. In our modern context, this sadly includes 'sex, drugs, and rock 'n' roll'.

If yin becomes extremely vacuous and yang fire becomes extremely hyperactive, yin and yang may come apart and fail to interact in a harmonious and healthy way. Water is yin and the kidneys are the water viscus according to theory in Chinese medicine known as five phase theory. Fire is yang and the heart is the fire viscus, such an extreme coming apart of yin and yang is sometimes referred to as heart and kidneys not interacting.

Heart vacuity and gallbladder timidity[3]

This mechanism of insomnia may often be seen in women who are somewhat overweight. Fat or adipose tissue is seen as abnormally accumulated phlegm, dampness and turbidity in Chinese medicine. Mostly, this is due to a spleen that is too weak to transform the digestate properly. The clear and turbid are not separated completely and turbid dampness lingers, accumulates and congeals into phlegm. Since the spleen qi is weak, the blood is not produced sufficiently to nourish the heart spirit, which becomes restless. Also, because the spleen qi is weak and insufficient, heart and lung qi are vacuous and weak. At the same time, due to emotional stress (and in Western culture, being overweight is itself a cause of stress and frustration), there is liver depression qi stagnation. When the depressed qi accumulates, because it is yang, it tends to counterflow upwards. When it counterflows upwards, it may draft phlegm along with it and this phlegm may confound or obstruct the orifices or portals of the heart. When such phlegm causes blockage of the flow of qi and blood to the heart, the spirit becomes even more upset and tends to stir frenetically like a drowning man gasping for air.

Thus this type of insomnia is due to a combination of weak spleen function resulting in heart vacuity on the one hand and phlegm accumulation on the other, plus emotional stress resulting in liver depression qi stagnation. While this type of

---

[3] In China, bravery is associated with the gallbladder. Because timidity and feeling frightened are the main symptoms of this pattern, it is called gallbladder timidity. However, it is the heart qi which is vacuous and weak and the liver qi which is depressed.

insomnia is mostly seen in women with a tendency to obesity, it is definitely aggravated by an incorrect diet and additional stress. Any food or drink which either damages the spleen or gives rise to even more phlegm and dampness will make this disease mechanism worse, as will any emotional stress or frustration making the person's liver more depressed and qi more stagnant.

Phlegm fire harassing the heart

This mechanism is essentially the same as the one above. However, in this case, depression has endured long enough or is severe enough for liver depression to turn into depressive heat or fire. Thus there is phlegm blocking the orifices of the heart at the same time as there is fire disturbing the heart spirit. Since the heart spirit is restless, yang qi cannot stop stirring and sinks downwards and into the enfolding womb of dark yin. Such depressive heat and phlegm are both aggravated by greasy, fatty fried foods, hot, acrid, peppery foods, and alcohol. This is in addition to the emotional upset which causes liver depression and the faulty diet which damages the spleen and subsequently promotes the creation of phlegm and dampness.

Stomach disharmony

It is also possible for simple overeating to cause insomnia. Typically, this type of insomnia is episodic and secondary to a particular meal which was too large and too late in the day. Food is yin and yin substance can hinder or block the free flow of yang. We have seen above that yang qi follows a daily diurnal cycle of moving upwards and outwards with the sun in the morning and downwards and inwards with the sun in the afternoon. The defensive qi is part of the yang qi in the body and it is this yang qi which is responsible for wakefulness. For sleep to come, the yang qi of the body, including the defensive qi, must travel to the deep interior of the body, away from the surface. If the stomach is full of solid, yin food, the diurnal

retreat of defensive yang away from the surface and upper parts
of the body is blocked. In this case, the food in the stomach may
literally block the yang qi from entering the interior of the body.
Remember that the stomach which is a bowel is more 'exterior'
than the viscera which are yin. If the yang qi gets hung up in the
stomach, it is still in a relatively yang part of the body and so
there is still consciousness. There is also likely to be a stomach
ache! Or at least abdominal fullness.

Blood stasis
The Chinese word for stasis is derived from the Chinese word
for silt. Therefore, static blood is seen as a kind of dry, dead or
wrecked blood which silts up and obstructs the channels and
vessels. Such blood stasis may be due to traumatic injury,
long-standing liver depression qi stagnation failing to move
the blood, qi vacuity failing to push the blood, cold
congealing the blood, or insufficient blood to nourish the
vessels and keep them open and functioning correctly. In
Chinese medicine, it is a given that static blood hinders the
creation of new or fresh blood. This means that blood stasis
may give rise to blood vacuity and blood vacuity may give rise
to blood stasis. Although no Chinese texts on insomnia list
blood stasis as one of the mechanisms of insomnia, since blood
vacuity may fail to nourish the heart spirit, and since
blood vacuity may lead to yin vacuity with attendant ascendant
hyperactivity of yang and heat or fire, blood stasis may
complicate many cases of insomnia, especially in women who
often have blood stasis in their uterus. Such female blood stasis
in the uterus is usually due to persistent liver depression qi
stagnation not moving the blood, which is in turn due to
emotional stress and frustration or to the after-effects of certain
medications and procedures, such as oral birth control pills,
abortions, tubal ligations, and pelvic inflammatory disease
treated by antibiotics alone.

As the reader can see, in Chinese medicine there are different causes and mechanisms for insomnia in different people. Some of the causes are age and body type related. Some have to do with mental-emotional causes and reactions. Some have to do with either too much or too little exercise and activity. Some may be due to other diseases in the body. Yet others may be due to faulty diet. Since not all people's insomnia is the same, no one treatment will be effective for everyone. More importantly, if one can identify their pattern of insomnia, one can immediately know what they as individuals should and should not do, eat or not eat. Further, because just the right treatment is given to the right individual, there is healing without side effects or doctor-caused complications.

THE CHINESE MEDICAL
TREATMENT OF INSOMNIA

Fundamental to Traditional Chinese Medicine, or TCM, is a concept known as 'treatment based on pattern discrimination'. Modern Western medicine bases its treatment on a disease diagnosis. This means that two patients diagnosed as suffering from the same disease will get the same treatment. Traditional Chinese Medicine also takes the patient's disease diagnosis into account, the choice of treatment is not based on the disease so much as it is on what is called the patient's pattern. It is this treatment based on pattern discrimination that makes this form of medicine holistic, safe, and effective.

In order to explain the difference between a disease and a pattern, let us take headache for example. All headaches, by definition, must involve some pain in the head. In modern Western medicine and other medical systems which primarily prescribe on the basis of a disease diagnosis, one can talk about 'headache medicines'. However, amongst headache sufferers, one may be a man and the other a woman. One may be old and the other young. One may be fat and the other skinny. One may have pain on the right side of her head and the other may have pain on the left. In one case, the pain may be throbbing and continuous, while the other person's pain may be very sharp but intermittent. In one case, they may also have indigestion, a tendency to loose stools, lack of warmth in their feet, red eyes, a dry mouth and desire for cold drinks, while the other person has a wet, weeping, crusty skin rash with red borders, a tendency to hay fever, ringing in their ears, and dizziness when they stand up. In Chinese medicine just as in modern Western medicine, both these patients suffer from headache. That is their disease diagnosis. However, they also suffer from a whole host of other complaints, have very different types of headaches, and very different constitutions, ages and sex. In Chinese medicine, the patient's pattern is made up from all these other signs and symptoms and other information. Thus, in Chinese medicine, the pattern describes *the totality of the person as a unique individual.* And in Chinese medicine, treatment is designed to rebalance that entire pattern of imbalance as well as address the major complaint or disease. Thus, there is a saying in Chinese medicine:

> One disease, different treatments
> Different diseases, same treatment

This means that, in Chinese medicine, two patients with the same named disease diagnosis may receive different treatments *if their Chinese medical patterns are different,* while two patients diagnosed with different named diseases may receive the same treatment *if their Chinese medical pattern is the same.* In other words, in Chinese medicine, treatment is predicated primarily on one's pattern discrimination, not on one's named disease diagnosis. Therefore, each person is treated individually.

Since every patient gets just the treatment which is right to restore balance to their particular body, there are also no unwanted side effects. Side effects come from forcing one part of the body to behave while causing an imbalance in some other part. The medicine may have fitted part of the problem but not the entirety of the patient as an individual. This is like robbing Peter to pay Paul. Since Chinese medicine sees the entire body (and mind!) as a single, unified whole, curing imbalance in one area of the body while causing it in another is unacceptable.

Below is a description of the major Chinese medical patterns at work in insomnia.

TREATMENT BASED ON
PATTERN DISCRIMINATION

Liver depression qi stagnation

Main symptoms: Irritability, pre-menstrual breast distension and pain, chest and side of the rib pain, lower abdominal distension and pain, discomfort in the epigastrium and stomach, diminished appetite, possible delayed menstruation whose amount is either scanty or profuse, darkish, stagnant menstrual blood, the menses unable to come easily, a normal or slightly dark tongue with thin, white fur, and a bowstring,[4] fine pulse.

Treatment principles: Course the liver and rectify the qi.

In actual fact, this pattern by itself does not cause insomnia and it also rarely occurs in the simple, textbook way presented above. However, it is rare to find a patient with insomnia who does not have at least an element of liver depression, and, in such cases, it is important to remedy this condition. Due to a reciprocal relationship between the liver and spleen, if the liver gets depressed, the spleen tends to become vacuous and damp at the same time and the stomach tends to become hot and dry. Since the spleen engenders and transforms the blood, liver depression with spleen vacuity often gives rise to blood vacuity as well. If this pattern endures or if there are other aggravating circumstances, such as ageing, menstruation or lactation, it may also evolve into liver depression with yin vacuity failing to nourish the viscera, meaning primarily failing to nourish the heart viscus and the spirit the heart houses within it.

_____

[4] There are 28 main pulse types in Chinese medicine, the bowstring pulse being one of these. It feels like its name implies – like a taut violin or bowstring.

Liver depression transforms heat

Main symptoms: All the above signs and symptoms plus the following differences. Firstly, the patient is not just irritable, they are downright angry. Secondly, there is a bitter taste in their mouth in the mornings when they wake. And third, there is yellow tongue fur and a bowstring, rapid pulse.

Treatment principles: Course the liver and rectify the qi, clear heat and resolve depression.

Heart–spleen dual vacuity

Main symptoms: Heart palpitations either before or after the menses or prompted or worsened by exercise and fatigue, loss of sleep, lassitude of the spirit, lack of strength, a slightly puffy face, the amount of the menses either profuse or scanty but pale in colour, a pale tongue with thin, white fur, and a soggy, small or fine, weak pulse.

Treatment principles: Supplement and nourish heart and spleen qi and blood.

Heart–spleen dual vacuity means heart blood vacuity and spleen qi vacuity. If heart blood is more vacuous, the amount of the menstruate is scanty. If spleen qi vacuity is more prominent, the amount of discharge is profuse. In both cases, the colour of the menstruate tends to be pale. Also, if the spleen is vacuous and, therefore, also damp, the pulse will be soggy.[5] But if blood is vacuous, the pulse will be fine. This pattern is also rarely, if ever, seen in its simple, discrete form in clinical practice. Commonly, if there is heart–blood vacuity, this merely complicates liver depression and spleen vacuity. If the liver depression is

---

[5] A soggy pulse is another of the main 28 pulse images of Chinese medicine. It refers to a pulse which is floating, fine and forceless.

secondary in importance, one would choose a guiding formula that primarily supplements and nourishes the heart and spleen, modifying it for liver depression. If liver depression is primary, then one would modify a formula from under that pattern.

Yin vacuity, fire effulgence

Main symptoms: Heart vexation, insomnia, heart palpitations worsened in the evening or due to stress, menstruation either early or late, lumbar soreness, numb extremities, one-sided headache, tinnitus, blurred vision, distension and pain that feels as if it stretches from the lower abdomen to the chest and breasts, frequent, short urination, length of menstruation short and amount profuse, a dry mouth with scanty fluids, a red tongue with scanty, shiny or peeled fur, and a fine, rapid, bowstring pulse.

Treatment principles: Supplement the kidneys and enrich yin, regulate the liver and bear down fire.

Although not stated in the Chinese title of this pattern, liver qi depression and stagnation are a part of this scenario. This is evidenced by the feeling of lower abdominal distension and pain reaching to the chest and breasts and also by the bowstring pulse.

Heart and kidneys not interacting

Main symptoms: Vexation and agitation, vexatious heat in the centre of the heart, restlessness, severe, continuous palpitations or racing heart, coolness of the lower limbs, great difficulty falling asleep, a red tongue with dry, yellow fur, and a fine, rapid or surging pulse.

Treatment principles: Clear the heart and lead yang to move downwards to its lower origin.

As discussed above, the pattern of heart and kidneys not interacting is an extreme form of yin vacuity with yang heat counterflowing upwards to accumulate and disturb the spirit residing in the heart.

Heart vacuity, gallbladder timidity
Main symptoms: Timidity, susceptibility to fright, fatigue, heart palpitations, shortness of breath, profuse dreaming, reduced sleep, waking in a startle or fright.

Treatment principles: Supplement the qi, nourish the heart, and quiet the gallbladder.

This pattern is actually fairly complex. Although the name of the pattern does not say this in so many words, there is spleen qi vacuity leading to a heart and lung qi vacuity on the one hand and an accumulation of dampness and phlegm on the other. There is also heart–blood vacuity and liver depression qi stagnation. When the treatment principles say to supplement the qi, this means the heart and lung qi which is essentially derived from the spleen qi. When we say to nourish the heart, this means to nourish the heart blood. And when we say to quiet the gallbladder, this means to course the liver and rectify the qi. Although the treatment principles do not say this, one must also eliminate dampness and transform phlegm.

Phlegm heat internally harassing
Main symptoms: Insomnia, a heavy, full, stuffy or tight feeling in the head, excessive or profuse phlegm, chest oppression,[6] aversion to food, burping and belching, acid regurgitation,

─────────────────────

[6] Chest oppression refers to a feeling of tightness and stuffiness in the chest. As a reaction to this feeling, the person will often sigh in an attempt to inhale fresh air and exhale the pent-up stale air.

possible nausea, heart vexation,[7] a bitter taste in the mouth, vertigo and dizziness, slimy, yellow tongue fur, and a slippery, rapid, possibly also bowstring pulse.

Treatment principles: Transform phlegm and clear heat, harmonise the centre and quiet the spirit.

As in the pattern above, this pattern's name and treatment principles do not completely describe the mechanisms causing these signs and symptoms. Harmonising the centre means to harmonise and regulate the bearing up and bearing down of the qi mechanism. The nausea, belching and acid regurgitation all evidence that there is upward counterflow. Most commonly, this upward counterflow is due to liver depression qi stagnation resulting in counterflow. If qi backs up and accumulates, eventually it must vent itself somewhere. Since it is yang, it typically vents itself upwards. In addition, extreme or enduring depression has transformed into heat or even fire.

Stomach disharmony
Main symptoms: Indigestion, no thought for or aversion at the thought of food, nausea, bad breath, thick, slimy tongue fur, and a slippery pulse.

Treatment principles: Harmonise the stomach and disperse food.

This pattern may be of recent onset due to a single bout of over-eating and drinking. In that case, it may be seen as a simple, discrete pattern as described above. However, this pattern may also complicate other patterns associated with either liver

_____

[7] Heart vexation refers to an irritating, possibly dry, hot sensation in the chest in front of the heart.

depression or phlegm. This is because the liver's control over coursing and discharging is intimately connected with the process of digestion by the stomach. Additionally, if there is liver depression qi stagnation and spleen vacuity giving rise to the accumulation of dampness and phlegm, it is even more likely that the stomach will become disharmonious. This means that often symptoms of food stagnating in the stomach, such as bad breath, nausea, indigestion, thick, slimy tongue fur and a slippery pulse, merely complicate other patterns. In this case, the treatment principles for other patterns are amended by the addition of the principles of harmonising the stomach and dispersing food or abducting stagnation. If the stomach qi is harmonised correctly, stagnant food will automatically be dispersed and abducted or led downwards to the intestines.

Blood stasis

Main symptoms: Pre-menstrual or menstrual lower abdominal pain which is either severe or is fixed in location and sharp or piercing in nature, varicose veins, chronic haemorrhoids, various types of lower abdominal lumps and masses, such as endometriosis, ovarian cysts and uterine fibroids, lumps in the breast, sharp, piercing pain anywhere in the body which is fixed in location and which tends to be worse in the evenings and night, a dark, dusky facial complexion or a tendency to brown spots on the skin, such as so-called age or liver spots, a purplish tongue or a tongue with static spots or static macules (i.e., black and blue patches), dark, engorged, twisted and prominent veins under the tongue, and a bowstring, fine, choppy pulse.[8]

---

[8] A choppy pulse means a pulse whose beat is not very regular. Although this pulse does not actually contain skipped beats, its beats tend to speed up and slow down. In addition, the force of each beat as it hits the fingertips may be variable, some beats being noticeably stronger than others.

Treatment principles: Quicken the blood and transform or dispel stasis.

This pattern is rarely encountered as the sole pattern accounting for a person's insomnia. Therefore, most clinical manuals do not even list it. However, blood stasis does commonly complicate many people's insomnia, especially insomnia in women and in the elderly. In cases complicated by insomnia, the treatment principles for blood stasis are then added to the other treatment principles and the treatment for blood stasis is then added to other treatments for other patterns.

THE REAL DEAL

Although textbook discriminations such as the one above make it seem like all the practitioner has to do is match up their patient's symptoms with one of the aforementioned patterns and then prescribe the recommended guiding formula, in actual clinical practice, one usually encounters combinations of discrete patterns and their related disease mechanisms or progressions. For instance, liver depression transforming heat may be complicated by spleen qi and heart blood vacuity. This, in turn may also be complicated by phlegm or blood stasis. Likewise, yin vacuity with fire effulgence may be complicated by liver depression and qi vacuity, liver depression and blood stasis, or liver depression and phlegm.

As insomnia itself is such a frustrating and stressful condition it will most likely lead to liver qi stagnation, even if this wasn't the initial cause.

Supporting the functioning of the liver in its role of spreading the qi is fundamental in the Chinese medical treatment of insomnia.

HOW THIS SYSTEM WORKS IN REAL LIFE

Using all the above information on the theory of Chinese medicine and the patterns and their mechanisms of insomnia, let's see how a Practitioner of Chinese Medicine makes this system work in real life.

JOCELYNE'S CASE

Take the case of Jocelyne, for instance, who was introduced at the beginning of this book. Let's look at her case in greater detail: she has had insomnia for several weeks and specifically, has been having trouble getting to sleep. Once she gets to sleep, she has many disturbing dreams and often finds herself waking in a panic. Jocelyne is 38 years old. She is somewhat overweight but has a very strong, fairly solid body. When Jocelyne gets under stress, she often feels a lump in the back of her throat as if there was something there which she could neither swallow down nor spit up. She describes this as 'postnasal drip' and says that she typically does hack up some white phlegm every morning when taking her shower. Jocelyne also says that she often has headaches which feel like a tight band around her head. Her chest feels stuffy and tight and she often sighs. When she really gets stressed, she feels some pain in her left chest or ribs. That scares her and she worries about having a heart attack. This fear of heart attack is worsened by the presence of heart palpitations when she gets nervous or stressed.

Lately, Jocelyne has noticed that she is frequently getting red, painful sores on the tip of her tongue and is waking with a bitter taste in her mouth. Also when she wakes, her mouth is very dry and she is very thirsty. Jocelyne's insomnia gets worse before her menstruation, at which time she also has sore, swollen breasts, lower abdominal distension, and a tendency to constipation which turns to diarrhoea on the first day of her period. She has had moderately painful cramps on the first day of her period for years, 'Doesn't everyone?' In general, Jocelyne says she is and has been depressed for a long time. When I ask her what depression means to her, she says it is a combination of feeling fatigued and irritable at the same time. When I ask her to stick out her tongue, it is somewhat redder than normal, especially on its tip and edges, and it has slightly dry, yellow, somewhat slimy fur or coating. Her pulse is bowstring, slippery and rapid, but also bowstring and soggy just over the wrist bone on her right hand.

HOW A CHINESE MEDICINE PRACTITIONER ANALYSES JOCELYNE'S SYMPTOMS

In Chinese medicine, difficulty falling asleep initially is usually due more to hyperactivity of yang than vacuity of yin or blood. The facts that Jocelyne is slightly overweight, has headaches like a tight band around her head, and has excessive phlegm all suggest that phlegm dampness is playing a part in her total pattern or picture. The feeling of phlegm in the back of her throat is called *plum pit* qi in Chinese medicine and is an indication of upwardly counterflowing phlegm lodged in the throat due to liver depression qi stagnation in turn due to stress. This is confirmed by Jocelyne's pre-menstrual breast distension and pain, chest and rib pain, pre-menstrual and menstrual lower abdominal pain, constipation before the onset of her menses, irritability and bowstring pulse, all of which when taken together in Chinese medicine are seen as emblems of liver depression qi stagnation. The bitter taste in her mouth in the morning shows that enduring or extreme depression has transformed into heat. This is confirmed by the red tongue tip and edges, the rapid pulse, the yellow tongue fur, and the sores on the tip of the tongue, all of which indicate heat. The slimy fur and the slippery pulse indicate phlegm. The loose stools at the onset of the menses, the fatigue, and the soggy pulse in the pulse position associated with the spleen all indicate that Jocelyne's phlegm is, in part, due to spleen qi vacuity not moving and transforming fluids which then gather and accumulate, first transforming into dampness and then congealing into phlegm.

Therefore, the Chinese Medicine Practitioner knows that there is phlegm fire due to a combination of liver depression transforming heat and spleen vacuity engendering dampness and then phlegm. The insomnia is thus due to phlegm confounding the portals of the heart at the same time as fire harasses the heart spirit. This leads to insomnia, heart palpitations and disturbing, profuse dreams.

HOW A CHINESE MEDICINE PRACTITIONER TREATS JOCELYNE'S INSOMNIA

Once the practitioner has ascertained the patient's pattern discrimination, the next step is to formulate the treatment principles necessary to rebalance the imbalance implied by this pattern discrimination. If phlegm fire or heat are listed as the main pattern, then the treatment principles are to transform phlegm and bear down fire or clear heat. If, secondarily, there is liver depression transforming heat, then the principles of coursing the liver and resolving depression would be added. Further, if phlegm is due to spleen vacuity not moving and transforming body fluids, then one should also fortify the spleen and supplement the qi.

Once the Chinese Medicine Practitioner has stated the treatment principles, then they know that anything which works to accomplish these principles will be good for the patient. Using these principles, the practitioner can now select various acupuncture points which achieve these effects. They can prescribe Chinese herbal medicinals which embody these principles. They can make recommendations about what to eat and what not to eat based on these principles. They can make recommendations on lifestyle changes. And, in short, they can advise the patient on *many aspects of their life*, judging whether something either aids the accomplishment of these principles or works against it.

In Chinese medicine, the internal administration of Chinese 'herbal' medicinals is one of the main treatments or therapies.[9] So let's look at how a Chinese Medicine Practitioner crafts a prescription for Jocelyne. Because the first treatment principle stated for Jocelyne is to transform phlegm, the Chinese herbalist knows that he or she should select their guiding formula from the phlegm-transforming category of formulas. Depending on the textbook, there are 22–28 main categories of formulas in Chinese medicine, each category correlated to a main treatment principle. The category of phlegm-transforming formulas is subdivided into formulas which transform and clear phlegm heat and those which transform and warm phlegm cold. Since Jocelyne's case has to do with phlegm fire, we need to pick a formula from those which transform phlegm and clear heat or fire.

Under this category of formulas, there are some formulas which mainly treat respiratory tract problems, such as bronchitis, pneumonia, asthma and whooping cough. Since Jocelyne's main complaint is insomnia, we must look for a formula which is empirically known through clinical experience to treat insomnia. Very quickly the list narrows down to one very famous formula, *Huang Lian Wen Dan Tang* (Coptis Warm the Gallbladder Decoction). This formula is for the treatment of insomnia, excessive fright and heart palpitations due to a

---

[9] I've put the word herbal in quotation marks since Chinese medicine is not entirely herbal. Herbs are medicinals made from parts of plants, their roots, bark, stems, leaves, flowers, etc. Chinese medicinals are mostly herbal in nature. However, a percentage of Chinese medicinals also come from the animal and mineral realms. Thus not all Chinese medicinals are, strictly speaking, herbs.

combination of liver depression transforming heat and phlegm harassing the heart. Since liver depression is already a part of this formula's rationale, we may not need to add anything more for the liver depression qi stagnation we have identified at work in Jocelyne. However, this formula does not include anything for fortifying the spleen and supplementing the qi. Therefore, we will have to add some ingredients for these purposes.

Hence the final formula composed by the Chinese herbalist will be called *Huang Lian Wen Dan Tang Jia Wei* (Coptis Warm the Gallbladder Decoction with Added Flavours [i.e., Ingredients]). This formula is comprised of:

Radix Codonopsitis Pilosulae (*Dang Shen*)
Rhizoma Coptidis Chinensis (*Huang Lian*)
Caulis Bambusae In Taeniis (*Zhu Ru*)
Rhizoma Pinelliae Teranatae (*Ban Xia*)
Sclerotium Poriae Cocos (*Fu Ling*)
Pericarpium Citri Reticulatae (*Chen Pi*)
Fructus Immaturus Citri Aurantii (*Zhi Shi*)
Radix Glycyrrhizae (*Gan Cao*)
uncooked Rhizoma Zingiberis (*Sheng Jiang*)

Radix Codonopsitis fortifies the spleen and supplements the qi. It is not part of the standard prescription but is added in order to take care of and embody those treatment principles having to do with Jocelyne's spleen qi vacuity which is connected with her engenderment of phlegm and dampness. Rhizoma Coptidis is bitter and cold and clears heat from the liver, stomach and heart. Therefore, it is very good for eliminating depressive heat affecting the heart but originating in the liver. Caulis Bambusae also clears depressive heat in the liver at the same time as it elimates vexation, that hot sense of irritability in the chest. Further, Caulis Bambusae bears down the stomach, thus bearing down the upwardly counterflowing depressive heat. Rhizoma Pinelliae likewise harmonises or bears down the stomach. It also transforms phlegm and eliminates dampness via the spleen's movement and transformation. Pinellia is aided in this by Sclerotium Poriae which fortifies the spleen and eliminates dampness via urination. Poria also supplements the heart qi and quiets the spirit. Pericarpium Citri is aged Orange or Tangerine Peel. It helps Pinellia transform phlegm dampness at the same time as it helps Bambusa regulate the bearing down of qi. Likewise Fructus Immaturus Citri, immature Aurantium fruit, even more strongly rectifies and regulates the qi. Together, these last two ingredients can help eliminate pre-menstrual breast distension due to liver depression qi stagnation. Radix Glycyrrhizae or Licorice supplements the spleen and heart. It also helps harmonise all the other ingredients in the formula and prevents them from having unwanted side effects. Uncooked Rhizoma Zingiberis or Ginger helps eliminate dampness and transform phlegm at the same time as it harmonises the stomach and promotes the movement of qi.

Hence one can see that the ingredients in this formula very precisely and specifically embody and carry out the treatment principles we have said were necessary for rebalancing Jocelyne's condition. To make this formula even more effective, the Chinese herbalist will often further modify the original formula by taking out one or more ingredients and adding others as necessary. This is done in order to tailor the formula to the individual patient's exact configuration of signs and symptoms. Since Jocelyne experiences pre-menstrual and menstrual abdominal cramping, I would first add Rhizoma Cyperi Rotundi (*Xiang Fu*) and Rhizoma Corydalis Yanhusuo (*Yan Hu Suo*) further to move the qi and stop pain. To eliminate the pre-menstrual breast distension and pain at the same time as quieting the spirit and improving the sleep, I would add Semen Citri Reticulatae (*Ju He*) and Cortex Albizziae Julibrissin (*He Huan Pi*). For the loose stools at the onset of the period, I might add Rhizoma Atractylodis Macrocephalae (*Bai Zhu*) to fortify the spleen even more and dry dampness. However, since depressive heat has damaged fluids somewhat, as evidenced by the thirst and dry mouth on waking in the morning, I would probably add Tuber Ophiopogonis Japonici (*Mai Dong*). This ingredient would not only enrich stomach fluids but also clear heat from the heart at the same time as transforming phlegm.

Usually, a formula such as this when used to treat insomnia would be taken two to three times each day. The herbs would be soaked in water and then boiled into a very strong 'tea' for 30–45 minutes. Since insomnia is Jocelyne's major complaint, I would probably have her begin taking this 'tea' at noon, with the third or last dose being taken a half-hour before bed in order to ensure its effect being strong and targeted for the second half of the day. Each week, I would check with Jocelyne to see how she was doing and if I needed to make any modifications to her formula. Remember, the Chinese herbalist wants to heal without causing *any* side-effects. If the formula does cause any unwanted effects, then it is my job to add and subtract ingredients until it achieves a perfect result with no unwanted effects.

The ingredients in this formula may also be taken as a dried, powdered extract. Such extracts are manufactured by several Taiwanese and Japanese companies. Although such extracts are not, in my experience, as powerful as the freshly decocted 'teas', they are easier to take. Many standard formulas also come as ready-made pills. However, these cannot be modified. If their ingredients match the individual patient's requirements, then they are fine. If the formula needs modifications, then teas or powders whose individual ingredients can be added and subtracted are necessary.

In exactly the same way, the Chinese Medicine Practitioner could create an individual acupuncture treatment plan and may create an accompanying dietary and lifestyle plan. We will discuss each of these in their own chapter. In a woman Jocelyne's age with her Chinese pattern discrimination, either Chinese herbal medicine alone, acupuncture alone, or a combination of the two supported by the proper diet and lifestyle will usually eliminate or at the very least drastically diminish her insomnia within three to five days. Often results will be apparent the first night after taking the herbs for a full day. However, the reader should understand that such Chinese medicinals are not like sedatives. One cannot simply take them at bedtime and expect to get a sound night's sleep. Chinese medicinals such as these act to restore balance and harmony to the yin and yang of the body. They do not usually provide immediate symptomatic relief to insomnia in the same way as taking a sleeping pill. They do not cause any drowsiness or grogginess the next day and may have many other beneficial effects on a person's health and well-being.

CHINESE HERBAL MEDICINE AND INSOMNIA

As we have seen from Jocelyne's case above, there is no Chinese 'insomnia herb' or even an 'insomnia formula' that will work for all sufferers of insomnia. Chinese medicinals are individually prescribed based on a person's pattern discrimination, not on a disease diagnosis like insomnia. Patients often come to me and say, 'My friend told me that *Tian Wang Bu Xin Dan* (Heavenly Emperor Supplement the Heart Elixir, a common Chinese over-the-counter medication) is good for insomnia. But I tried it and it didn't work.' This is because *Tian Wang Bu Xin Dan* is meant to treat a *specific pattern* of insomnia, not insomnia per se. If you exhibit that pattern, then this formula will work. If you do not have signs and symptoms of this pattern, it won't.

Also, because most people's insomnia is a combination of different Chinese patterns and disease mechanisms, Chinese medicine never treats insomnia with a single herb. Chinese herbal medicine is based on rebalancing patterns, and patterns in real-life patients almost always have more than a single element. Therefore, Chinese herbalists almost always prescribe herbs in multi-ingredient formulas. Such formulas may have anywhere from three to eighteen or more ingredients. When a Chinese herbalist reads a prescription given by another practitioner, they can tell you not only what the patient's pattern discrimination is but also their probable signs and symptoms. In other words, the Chinese herbalist does not just combine several medicinals that are all reputed to be 'good for insomnia'. Rather, they carefully craft a formula whose ingredients are meant to rebalance every aspect of the patient's body-mind. In this way the insomnia will be treated.

TRADITIONAL CHINESE HERBAL REMEDIES

In this chapter we will look closely at some traditional Chinese herbal formulas which are available in a prepared form, either powders or pills. These remedies have been used for centuries to effectively treat people with insomnia.

We have included these herbal formulas to give you a deeper understanding of how Chinese herbal medicine works, rather than as a self-help guide.

In the UK it is not possible to buy Chinese herbal medicines unless you have a prescription from a trained practitioner. We would strongly recommend that you seek professional advice when taking Chinese herbs.

Xiao Yao Wan (also spelled *Hsiao Yao Wan*)

Xiao Yao Wan[10] is one of the most common Chinese herbal formulas prescribed. Its Chinese name has been translated as Free and Easy Pills, Rambling Pills, Relaxed Wanderer Pills, and several other versions of this same idea of promoting a freer and smoother, more relaxed flow.

The ingredients in this formula are:

Radix Bupleuri (*Chai Hu*)
Radix Angelicae Sinensis (*Dang Gui*)
Radix Albus Paeoniae Lactiflorae (*Bai Shao*)
Rhizoma Atractylodis Macrocephalae (*Bai Zhu*)
Sclerotium Poriae Cocos (*Fu Ling*)
mix-fried Radix Glycyrrhizae (*Gan Cao*)
Herba Menthae Haplocalycis (*Bo He*)
uncooked Rhizoma Zingiberis (*Sheng Jiang*)

---

[10] This formula is also known as Bupleurum and Tang-kuei Formula.

This formula treats the pattern of liver depression qi stagnation complicated by blood vacuity and spleen weakness with possible dampness as well. Bupleurum courses the liver and rectifies the qi. It is aided in this by Herba Menthae Haplocalycis or Peppermint. Dang Gui and Radix Albus Paeoniae Lactiforae or White Peony nourish the blood and soften and harmonise the liver. Rhizoma Atractylodis Macrocephalae or Atractylodes and Sclerotium Poriae Cocos or Poria fortify the spleen and eliminate dampness. Mix-fried Licorice aids these two in fortifying the spleen and supplementing the liver, while uncooked Ginger aids in both promoting and regulating the qi flow and eliminating dampness.

When insomnia presents with the signs and symptoms of liver depression, spleen qi vacuity and an element of blood vacuity this formula may be very effective.

Dan Zhi Xiao Yao Wan

Dan Zhi Xiao Yao Wan or Moutan and Gardenia Rambling Pills is a modification of the previous formula.[11] It is meant to treat the pattern of liver depression transforming into heat with spleen vacuity and possible blood vacuity and/or dampness. The ingredients in this formula are the same as above except that two other herbs are added:

Cortex Radicis Moutan (*Dan Pi*)
Fructus Gardeniae Jasminoidis (*Shan Zhi Zi*)

These two ingredients clear heat and resolve depression. In addition, Cortex Radicis Moutan, or Moutan, quickens the blood and dispels stasis and is good at clearing heat specifically from the blood. Some Chinese Medicine Practitioners prefer to take out uncooked Ginger and Mint, while others leave these two ingredients in.

---

[11] This formula is also known as Bupleurum and Peony Formula.

Basically, the signs and symptoms of the pattern for which this formula is designed are the same as those for *Xiao Yao Wan* above plus signs and symptoms of depressive heat. These might include a reddish tongue with slightly yellow fur, a bowstring and rapid pulse, a bitter taste in the mouth, and increased irritability.

Suan Zao Ren Tang

Suan Zao Ren Tang (Zizyphus Seed Decoction)[12] treats insomnia and mental unrest due to liver blood vacuity. It can, therefore, be combined with *Xiao Yao Wan* when liver blood vacuity is more severe and manifests primarily as insomnia. Its ingredients are:

Semen Zizyphi Spinosae (*Suan Zao Ren*)
Sclerotium Poriae Cocos (*Fu Ling*)
Radix Ligustici Wallichii (*Chuan Xiong*)
Rhizoma Anemarrhenae Aspheloidis (*Zhi Mu*)
mix-fried Radix Glycyrrhizae (*Gan Cao*)

Gui Pi Wan (also spelled Kuei Pi Wan)

Gui means to return or restore, *pi* means the spleen, and *wan* means pills. Therefore, the name of this formula means Restore the Spleen Pills.[13] However, these pills not only supplement the spleen qi but also nourish heart blood and calm the heart spirit. They are the textbook guiding formula for the pattern of heart-spleen dual vacuity. In this case, there are symptoms of spleen qi vacuity, such as fatigue, poor appetite and cold hands and feet plus symptoms of heart blood vacuity, such as a pale tongue, heart palpitations and insomnia. This formula is also the standard one for treating heavy or abnormal bleeding due to the spleen not containing and restraining the blood within its

_____

[12] This formula is also known as Zizyphus Combination.

vessels. Therefore, this formula can be combined with *Xiao Yao Wan* when there is liver depression qi stagnation complicated by heart–blood and spleen qi vacuity. Its ingredients are:

Radix Astragali Membranacei (*Huang Qi*)
Radix Codonopsitis Pilosulae (*Dang Shen*)
Rhizoma Atractylodis Macrocephalae (*Bai Zhu*)
Sclerotium Parardicis Poriae Cocos (*Fu Shen*)
mix-fried Radix Glycyrrhizae (*Gan Cao*)
Radix Angelicae Sinensis (*Dang Gui*)
Semen Zizyphi Spinosae (*Suan Zao Ren*)
Arillus Euphoriae Longanae (*Long Yan Rou*)
Radix Polygalae Tenuifoliae (*Yuan Zhi*)
Radix Auklandiae Lappae (*Mu Xiang*)

Tian Wang Bu Xin Dan

The name of this formula translates as Heavenly Emperor's Supplement the Heart Elixir.[14] It treats insomnia, restlessness, fatigue and heart palpitations due to yin, blood and qi vacuity, with an emphasis on heart yin and liver blood vacuity. Its ingredients include:

uncooked Radix Rehmanniae (*Sheng Di*)
Radix Scrophulariae Ningpoensis (*Xuan Shen*)
Fructus Schisandrae Chinensis (*Wu Wei Zi*)
Tuber Asparagi Cochinensis (*Tian Men Dong*)
Tuber Ophiopogonis Japonici (*Mai Men Dong*)
Radix Angelicae Sinensis (*Dang Gui*)
Semen Biotae Orientalis (*Bai Zi Ren*)
Semen Zizyphi Spinosae (*Suan Zao Ren*)
Radix Salviae Miltiorrhizae (*Dan Shen*)

---

[13] This formula is also called Ginseng and Longan Combination.

[14] This formula is also called Ginseng and Zizyphus Formula.

Radix Polygalae Tenuifoliae (*Yuan Zhi*)
Sclerotium Poriae Cocos (*Fu Ling*)
Radix Codonopsitis Pilosulae (*Dang Shen*)

***Bai Zi Yang Xin Wan* (also spelled *Pai Tsu Yang Xin Wan*)**
The name of this formula translates as Biotae Nourish the Heart Pills. This formula is for heart yin and liver blood vacuity complicated by an element of phlegm obstruction. Its ingredients include:

Semen Biotae Orientalis (*Bai Zi Ren*)
Fructus Lycii Chinensis (*Gou Qi Zi*)
Radix Scrophulariae Ningpoensis (*Xuan Shen*)
uncooked Radix Rehmanniae (*Sheng Di*)
Tuber Ophiopogonis Japonici (*Mai Men Dong*)
Radix Angelicae Sinensis (*Dang Gui*)
Sclerotium Poriae Cocos (*Fu Ling*)
Rhizoma Acori Graminei (*Shi Chang Pu*)
Radix Glycyrrhizae (*Gan Cao*)

Bu Nao Wan
Similar to the above two formulas, Supplement the Brain Pills are another popular Chinese remedy for insomnia, restlessness, heart palpitations and poor memory. Their name is popularly mis- or overtranslated as Cerebral Tonic Pills. The pattern they are designed to remedy is a yin and yang vacuity, with emphasis on the blood and yin vacuity, plus internal stirring of wind due to yin vacuity with upward counterflow confounding or obstructing the portals of the heart. In this case, there is most likely also an element of liver depression which this formula does address.

We have not previously mentioned internal stirring of wind as a cause or type of insomnia. Internal stirring of wind here refers to upwardly counterflowing yang qi which is moving extremely frenetically or recklessly. It is indicated by dizziness and vertigo, tremors and spasms, and a quivering tongue. Besides insomnia, other conditions associated with this group of disease mechanisms are epilepsy, apoplexy, mania and seizures. Although there are no particular signs of heat or fire, the symptoms of ascendant liver wind are pronounced. The ingredients in this formula are:

Fructus Schisandrae Chinensis (*Wu Wei Zi*)
Semen Zizyphi Spinosae (*Suan Zao Ren*)
Radix Angelicae Sinensis (*Dang Gui*)
Fructus Lycii Chinensis (*Gou Qi Zi*)
Herba Cistanchis Deserticolae (*Rou Cong Rong*)
Semen Juglandis Regiae (*Hu Tao Ren*)
Semen Biotae Orientalis (*Bai Zi Ren*)
Rhizoma Acori Graminaei (*Shi Chang Pu*)
Rhizoma Arisaematis (*Nan Xing*)
Radix Gastrodiae Elatae (*Tian Ma*)
Succinum (*Hu Po*)
Dens Draconis (*Long Chi*)
Radix Polygalae Tenuifoliae (*Yuan Zhi*)

An Shen Bu Xin Wan (also spelled *An Shen Pu Shin Wan*)
An shen means to quiet the spirit. *Bu xin* means to supplement the heart. Therefore, the Chinese name for this formula means Quiet the Spirit and Supplement the Heart Pills. It is designed to treat insomnia, dizziness, restlessness, profuse dreaming which disturbs the sleep, and heart palpitations due to yin and blood vacuity. The ingredients also take into account an element of liver depression qi stagnation and an element of phlegm obstruction. In addition, because the ingredient with the largest dose in this formula is Mother of Pearl Powder, this formula helps to bear down upwardly counterflowing yang qi and quiet the spirit quite strongly. All its ingredients are:

Concha Maragaritiferae (*Zhen Zhu Mu*)
Radix Polygoni Multiflori (*He Shou Wu*)
Fructus Ligustri Lucidi (*Nu Zhen Zi*)
Herba Ecliptae Prostratae (*Han Lian Cao*)
Semen Cuscutae Chinensis (*Tu Si Zi*)
Fructus Schisandrae Chinensis (*Wu Wei Zi*)
Radix Salviae Miltiorrhizae (*Dan Shen*)
Cortex Albizziae Julibrissin (*He Huan Pi*)
Rhizoma Acori Graminei (*Shi Chang Pu*)

Jiang Ya Wan (also spelled *Chiang Ya Wan*)

Jiang ya means to decrease pressure as in high blood pressure. *Wan* as we've seen before means pills. These pills are usually used to treat high blood pressure due to kidney vacuity and liver effulgence. The reader should remember that actually Chinese medicine treats patterns of imbalance, not diseases such as high blood pressure. Also remember the saying, 'Different diseases, same treatment.' Therefore, these pills can be used to treat insomnia due to an upward flaring of liver fire or wind in turn due to loss of control by kidney yin below. Since this formula already includes medicinals for treating the liver, it would not be combined with *Xiao Yao Wan* above but used by itself. Its ingredients are:

Semen Leonuri Heterophyli (*Chong Wei Zi*)
Rhizoma Coptidis Chinensis (*Huang Lian*)
Cornu Antelopis Saiga-tatarici (*Ling Yang Jiao*)
Spica Prunellae Vulgaris (*Xia Ku Cao*)
Ramulus Uncariae Cum Uncis (*Gou Teng*)
Radix Gastrodiae Elatae (*Tian Ma*)
Succinum (*Hu Po*)
Radix Angelicae Sinensis (*Dang Gui*)
Radix Ligustici Wallichii (*Chuan Xiong*)
uncooked Radix Rehmanniae (*Sheng Di*)
Gelatinum Corii Asini (*E Jiao*)

Cortex Radicis Moutan (*Dan Pi*)
Radix Achyranthis Bidentatae (*Niu Xi*)
Lignum Aquilariae Agallochae (*Chen Xiang*)
Radix Et Rhizoma Rhei (*Da Huang*)

Because this formula contains Radix Et Rhizoma Rhei or Rhubarb which is a strong purgative, it should not be taken if one has diarrhoea or loose stools. If this formula causes diarrhoea, its use should be discontinued.

Kang Ning Wan

Kang means health and *ning* means tranquil. Therefore, *Kang Ning Wan* means Healthy Tranquillity Pills, although they are mistakenly known as Curing Pills. They are commonly used as a treatment for indigestion due to overeating and food stagnation. When insomnia is caused by overeating and overdrinking, one can take these pills before going to bed. Their ingredients are:

Semen Coicis Lachryma-jobi (*Yi Yi Ren*)
Cortex Magnoliae Officinalis (*Hou Po*)
Rhizoma Atractylodis (*Cang Zhu*)
Herba Agastachis Seu Pogostemi (*Huo Xiang*)
Radix Puerariae (*Ge Gen*)
Radix Angelicae Dahuricae (*Bai Zhi*)
Radix Auklandiae Lappae (*Mu Xiang*)
Massa Medica Fermentata (*Shen Qu*)
Radix Trichosanthis Kirlowii (*Tian Hua Fen*)
Fructus Germinatus Oryzae Sativae (*Gu Ya*)
Sclerotium Poriae Cocos (*Fu Ling*)
Rhizoma Gastrodiae Elatae (*Tian Ma*)
Flos Chrysanthemi Morifolii (*Ju Hua*)
Herba Menthae Haplocalycis (*Bo He*)
Pericarpium Citri Reticulatae (*Chen Pi*)

When food stagnation complicates liver depression qi stagnation or liver depression transforming heat, these pills may be combined with *Xiao Yao Wan* or *Dan Zhi Xiao Yao Wan* discussed previously.

Er Chen Wan

Er Chen Wan means Two Aged (Ingredients) Pills.[15] This is because two of its main ingredients are aged before using. This formula is used to transform phlegm and eliminate dampness. It can be added to *Xiao Yao Wan* if there is liver depression with spleen vacuity and more pronounced phlegm and dampness. If there is liver depression transforming heat giving rise to phlegm heat, it can be combined with *Dan Zhi Xiao Yao Wan*. Its ingredients include:

Rhizoma Pinelliae Ternatae (*Ban Xia*)
Sclerotium Poriae Cocos (*Fu Ling*)
mix-fried Radix Glycyrrhizae (*Gan Cao*)
Pericarpium Citri Reticulatae (*Chen Pi*)
uncooked Rhizoma Zingiberis (*Sheng Jiang*)

Tong Jing Wan (also spelled To Jing Wan)

The name of these pills means Painful Menstruation Pills. They are not an 'insomnia pill' per se. However, insomnia is often complicated by blood stasis in women and the elderly. Therefore, this pill can be taken along with other appropriate formulas when blood stasis is an important factor in someone's insomnia. Its ingredients are:

Tuber Curcumae (*Yu Jin*)
Rhizoma Sparganii (*San Leng*)
Radix Rubrus Paeoniae Lactiflorae (*Chi Shao*)

_____

15 When sold as a dried, powdered extract, this formula is called Citrus and Pinellia Combination.

Radix Angelicae Sinensis (*Dang Gui*)
Radix Ligustici Wallichii (*Chuan Xiong*)
Radix Salviae Miltiorrhizae (*Dan Shen*)
Flos Carthami Tinctorii (*Hong Hua*)

We have seen in this chapter how traditional Chinese herbal formulas are used to treat insomnia, working not on relieving the symptoms directly but rather by addressing underlying imbalances within the person. Different people are given different treatment depending on their underlying imbalances, so this approach contrasts with the use of sedatives and tranquillisers given in Western medicine regardless of the cause.

Should you wish to try Chinese herbal medicines or patents we will list the relevant professional bodies in a later chapter so that you may find a practitioner locally.

SIX GUIDEPOSTS FOR ASSESSING MEDICATIONS

In general, you can tell if any medication and treatment are beneficial for you by checking the following six guideposts.

1. Digestion	4. Mood
2. Elimination	5. Appetite
3. Energy level	6. Sleep

If a medication, be it Western or Chinese, improves your symptoms and these six basic mechanisms also improve, it is likely to be good treatment. However, if a medication causes deterioration in any of these six mechanisms, even if the symptoms improve it is probably not the correct treatment and certainly should not be taken on any long-term basis.

Chinese medicine tries to re-balance the body's energies and create harmony, allowing the body's own natural healing mechanisms to be reinstated. Nothing is more powerful than Nature's own healing.

ACUPUNCTURE, MOXIBUSTION AND ORIENTAL MEDICAL MASSAGE

n the previous chapters we have looked at the underlying causes of insomnia from a Traditional Chinese
Medicine point of view and its treatment with internal
or herbal medicine. This chapter will focus on how Chinese
medicine treats insomnia using acupuncture, moxibustion and
Oriental medical massage. Chinese medicine as it is practised
in modern China has evolved in a different social and cultural
context to the West and there are differences in how it is
practised. In modern China herbal treatment is very popular,
in fact Traditional Chinese Medicine (TCM) has evolved
principally from a herbal tradition. In the West there have been
many other influences and whilst TCM has played an important
role, other countries such as Japan have also been influential.
Shiatsu, for example, a type of Oriental medical massage
originating from Japan, is very popular in the West today and
can be an excellent therapy for insomnia. Acupuncture is
probably the most well known and widely practised form of
Chinese medicine in the UK, having been practised since the
1960s. It has grown enormously in popularity and there are now
many trained practitioners all over the country. We will give
details on how to find a properly qualified practitioner later on
in the book.

WHAT IS ACUPUNCTURE?

Acupuncture primarily means the insertion of extremely thin,
sterilised, stainless steel needles into specific points on the body
where there are special concentrations of qi and blood. These

points have a special regulatory influence and balance the flow of qi and blood over the channel and network system we described above. As we have seen, insomnia is due to a breakdown in the harmony between yin and yang in the body, and, in the human body, yin and yang ultimately mean the qi and blood. As we have also seen, there really is no insomnia if there is not also liver depression. Either liver depression is intimately connected with the mechanisms of insomnia to begin with, or due to the frustration and stress of insomnia, one subsequently develops liver depression. Liver depression means that the qi is stagnant. Since the qi is depressed and stagnant, it is not flowing when and where it should. Instead it counterflows or vents itself to areas of the body where it shouldn't be, attacking other organs and body tissues and making them dysfunctional.

Therefore, the Chinese patterns of insomnia typically include many signs and symptoms associated with lack of, or erroneous, counterflow qi flow. In addition, the heart spirit is said to be an accumulation of qi within the heart. If there is enough qi in the heart, then there is consciousness or what Chinese medicine calls the spirit. Since one of the main strengths of acupuncture is the ability to regulate and rectify the flow of qi, it is a highly appropriate therapy for treating insomnia.

As a generic term, acupuncture also includes several other methods of stimulating acupuncture points, thus regulating the flow of qi in the body. The main other modality is moxibustion. This is the warming of acupuncture points mainly by burning dried, aged Oriental Mugwort on, near or over the points. The purposes of this warming treatment are to 1) stimulate the flow of qi and blood even more strongly, 2) add warmth to areas of the body that are too cold, and 3) add yang qi to the body to supplement a yang qi deficiency. Other acupuncture modalities are to apply suction cups over points, to massage the points, to prick the points to allow a drop or two of blood to exit, to apply Chinese medicinals to the points, to apply magnets to the points, and to stimulate the points by either electricity or laser.

WHAT IS A TYPICAL ACUPUNCTURE TREATMENT ?

There are quite a few different styles or methods of practising acupuncture so some aspects of treatment will vary from practitioner to practitioner depending on their training. However, there are certain aspects which remain the same: all practitioners will take a case history and gather together information so that they can make a diagnosis; they will also use various methods to make an Oriental medical diagnosis; they will almost certainly take the pulse at the wrist; and they may examine the tongue and abdomen.

Once the diagnosis has been made the treatment will begin and very fine stainless steel needles will be inserted into selected points on the body. It is unusual for more than 15 needles to be inserted during a treatment so you won't end up looking like a pin cushion! The needles used are generally disposable, and if not they are sterilised according to hospital safety standards. There is no need to be concerned about infection as a properly trained acupuncturist who is a member of the relevant professional body must comply with strict standards of safety. The needles may be manipulated gently after insertion and they may be left in for up to 30 minutes until the acupuncturist feels the desired effect has been achieved. Some practitioners may use an electro-acupuncture machine, which is attached to the needles, to further stimulate the qi or energy flow.

Moxibustion may also be used, either on the needles or directly on the skin, and whatever the technique it is normally a pleasant, warm sensation and will not burn the patient.

HOW ARE THE ACUPUNCTURE
POINTS SELECTED?

The points the acupuncturist chooses to needle for each treatment are selected on the basis of Chinese medical theory and the known clinical effects of certain points. Since there are different schools or styles of acupuncture, point selection will vary from practitioner to practitioner. Let me present a fairly typical case from the point of view of one of the main methods of practising.

Let's say the patient's main complaints are difficulty falling asleep, irritability, fatigue, heart palpitations on exertion, shortness of breath and loose stools. Their tongue is swollen and pale with thin, white fur. Their tongue is so swollen that one can clearly see the indentations of the teeth on the edges of the tongue. Their pulse is fine and bowstring. This person's pattern discrimination is liver depression with heart–spleen dual vacuity. This is a very commonly encountered pattern of disharmony in women with insomnia in their 30s.

The treatment principles necessary for remedying this case are to course the liver and rectify the qi, fortify the spleen and nourish the heart, and quiet the spirit. In order to accomplish these aims, the practitioner might select the following points:

Tai Chong (Liver 3) Supreme Rushing
San Yin Jiao (Spleen 6) Three Yin Crossing
Zu San Li (Stomach 36) Leg Three Miles
Shen Men (Heart 7) Spirit Gate
Nei Guan (Pericardium 6) Inner Frontier Gate
Shan Zhong (Conception Vessel 17) Within the Breast
Bai Hui (Governing Vessel 20) One Hundred Meetings
Xin Shu (Bladder 15) Heart Correspondence
Pi Shu (Bladder 20) Spleen Correspondence

THE ACUPUNCTURE POINTS

As Chinese is a pictorial language rich in imagery I thought it might be helpful to include some English translations of the point names. Although each point is thought to have numerous effects on the person's energy, I feel the point names can convey some of the overall 'sense' or 'feeling' of the point and why it might have been chosen in this case.

Tai Chong

As the English name for this point, Supreme Rushing, suggests, it is tremendously helpful in moving stuck or blocked energies.

Tai Chong courses the liver and resolves depression, moves and rectifies the qi. Since liver depression qi stagnation is a main disease mechanism either causing or contributing to this patient's insomnia, this is a main or ruling point in this treatment. Since their easy anger or irritability stems from liver depression, this point also eliminates the source of their vexation.

San Yin Jiao

As the English name for this point, Three Yin Crossing, might suggest, it is an important point in regulating the yin energies of the body, which as we have seen are often out of balance in insomnia.

San Yin Jiao is chosen to further course the liver at the same time as it fortifies the spleen. It does both these things because both the liver and spleen channels cross at this point. Further, this point is known to promote the nourishment and supplementation of yin blood.

Zu San Li

The English name for this point is Leg Three Miles. It is an important centre of energy and can therefore bring great relief to someone who is suffering from insomnia and may be deeply tired or fatigued due to lack of sleep.

Zu San Li is a very powerful point on the stomach channel. Because the stomach is yang and the spleen is yin and because the stomach and spleen share a mutually 'exterior/interior' relationship, stimulating *Zu San Li* can bolster the spleen with yang qi from the stomach, which usually has plenty to spare. In addition, the stomach channel traverses the chest and, therefore, needling this point can regulate the qi in the chest. Since the heart gets its qi from the spleen, supplementing the spleen by way of the stomach is an acupuncture way of transferring qi from the stomach to the spleen and thence to the heart.

Shan Zhong

This is located at the level of the nipples on the chest bone between the breasts. It is a local point for freeing the flow of qi in the chest. It also helps calm the spirit and provides emotional relief.

Shen Men

This is a point on the heart channel which supplements the heart and quiets the spirit, and its English name is Spirit Gate. *Nei Guan* is a point on the pericardium channel. The pericardium is sometimes known as the heart protector, and supporting it may be important for someone who is under a lot of stress or going through emotional turmoil. Needling this point can have a very calming effect on the person. These two points are frequently selected to treat people suffering with insomnia.

Bai Hui

A point on the governing vessel, it is located at the very crown of the head. Therefore, it is the most yang point on the body. Needling it can quiet the spirit and push yang qi back downwards. It is also a very commonly used point for treating various patterns of insomnia.

Xin Shu and *Pi Shu*

These are points on the back associated with the heart and spleen respectively. They directly connect with these two viscera and can supplement weakness and deficiencies in these two organs.

This combination of nine acupuncture points treats the root causes of this patient's insomnia. It remedies both the underyling disease mechanism or energetic imbalance and addresses certain key symptoms in a very direct way. It is highly likely that after a few treatments with acupuncture the patient would not only see an improvement in their insomnia but their overall health and sense of well-being could be much improved.

DOES ACUPUNCTURE HURT?

In Chinese, it is said that acupuncture is *bu tong*, painless. However, patients may feel some mild soreness, heaviness, electrical tingling or distension. For most people the sensation is acceptable and not really painful although needle techniques vary and people do have different pain thresholds.

HOW QUICKLY WILL I FEEL THE RESULT?

One of the best things about the acupuncture treatment of insomnia is that its effects are often immediate. Since many of the mechanisms of insomnia have to do with stuck qi, as soon as the qi is made to flow, the symptoms disappear. So, many patients sleep better after the very first treatment.

In addition, because irritability and nervous tension are also mostly due to liver depression qi stagnation, some people will feel an immediate relief of irritability and tension while still on the treatment couch. Typically, you will feel quite tranquil and relaxed after insertion of the needles. Some patients drop off to sleep for a few minutes. It is very likely that you will feel relaxed after the treatment.

WHO SHOULD RECEIVE ACUPUNCTURE?

Acupuncture is generally an excellent treatment for insomnia as its effects are usually relatively immediate. Acupuncture is considered to be particularly effective in cases where there is stagnation of the qi and blood. If, however, there is a severe lack of qi and blood then acupuncture alone may not be as effective as internally administered Chinese herbal medicine. This is because acupuncture does not actually add anything to the body although it may improve the functioning of the various viscera and bowels which create qi and blood. If the insomnia is due to a severe lack of qi and blood then treatment with Chinese herbs may be more appropriate and this may be combined with acupuncture.

EAR ACUPUNCTURE

Some acupuncturists may also use points in the ear to treat insomnia. Needles may be used during the acupuncture session to stimulate specific points on the ear. Alternatively tiny metal pellets, seeds or special press needles are used which are covered with adhesive plaster or micropore and may be left in for a few days to support the treatment. In this way the duration and effectiveness of treatment may be enhanced.

ORIENTAL MEDICAL MASSAGE

Medical massage in China is called *tui na*. It has developed into a high art and is practised extensively in hospitals, where there is often a special ward or clinic within the hospital devoted to it. Like acupuncture it works on the meridian or channel system, and specific strokes or manipulations move and regulate the flow of qi. At present there are not many pracititioners of *tui na* in the UK, although it is growing in popularity.

Another form of Oriental medical massage is shiatsu which originates from Japan. This is a deeply relaxing therapy and there are quite a number of practitioners working in the UK. Shiatsu is done with the patient/client wearing loose, comfortable clothing. Diagnosis is mainly through gently palpating the abdomen to detect underlying imbalances in the person's energy. The relevant meridians or channels are then worked on to release blockages and strengthen areas of deficiency or vacuity. It may be a highly beneficial treatment for insomnia. Details of how to find a shiatsu practitioner will be given later on in the book.

THE THREE FREE THERAPIES

All the therapies and treatments of Chinese medicine we have so far described require the help and guidance of a professional practitioner. This chapter will focus on what you yourself can do, what I call the three free therapies. These are diet, exercise and deep relaxation and only you can take care of these three factors which are so important for your health and well-being.

DIET PRINCIPLES

In Chinese medicine, the function of the spleen and stomach are likened to a pot on a stove or a still. The stomach receives the foods and liquids which then 'rotten and ripen' like a mash in a fermentation vat. The spleen then cooks this mash and drives off (i.e., transforms and bears up) the pure part. This pure part collects in the lungs to become the qi and in the heart to become the blood. In addition, Chinese medicine characterises this transformation as a process of yang qi transforming yin substance. All the principles of Chinese dietary therapy, including what persons with insomnia should and should not eat, are derived from these basic concepts.

We have already seen that the spleen is at the root of qi and blood engenderment and transformation. Based on this concept, a healthy, strong spleen prevents and treats insomnia in three ways. Firstly, if the spleen is healthy and strong, it will create sufficient qi to push the blood and move body fluids. Therefore, a sufficiency of pushing or moving spleen qi helps counterbalance or control any tendency of the liver to constrict or constrain the qi flow. Thus, in Chinese medicine, a healthy spleen helps keeps the liver in check and free from depression and stagnation. Secondly, since the spleen is the root of blood production and it is yin blood which keeps yang qi in check, a healthy, strong spleen manufacturing abundant blood ensures a sufficiency of blood to nourish and quiet the spirit which is said to reside in the heart. And thirdly, since any qi, but especially blood, remaining unused at the end of the day can be converted into essence during sleep at night, a strong, healthy spleen manufacturing abundant qi and blood also helps ensure the bolstering and supplementation of yin by acquired essence.

Therefore, when it comes to Chinese dietary therapy and insomnia, there are two main issues: 1) to avoid foods which damage the spleen, and 2) to eat foods which help build yin and blood.

FOODS WHICH DAMAGE THE SPLEEN

In terms of foods which damage the spleen, Chinese medicine begins with uncooked, chilled foods. If the process of digestion is likened to cooking, then cooking is nothing other than pre-digestion outside of the body. In Chinese medicine, it is a given that the overwhelming majority of all food should be cooked, i.e., pre-digested. Although cooking may destroy some vital nutrients (in Chinese, qi), cooking does render the remaining nutrients much more easily assimilable. Therefore, even though some nutrients have been lost, the net absorption of nutrients is greater with cooked foods than raw. Further, eating raw foods makes the spleen work harder and thus wears the spleen out more quickly. If one's spleen is very robust, eating uncooked, raw foods may not be so damaging, but we have already seen that many women's spleens are already weak because of their monthly menses overtaxing the spleen *vis à vis* blood production. It is also a fact of life that the spleen typically becomes weak with age.

More importantly, chilled foods directly damage the spleen. Chilled and frozen foods and drinks neutralise the spleen's yang qi. The process of digestion is the process of turning all foods and drinks to 100°F soup within the stomach so that it may undergo distillation. If the spleen expends too much yang qi just warming the food up, then it will become damaged and weak. Therefore, all foods and liquids should be eaten and drunk at room temperature at the least and better at body temperature. The more signs and symptoms of spleen vacuity a person presents, such as fatigue, chronically loose stools, undigested food in the stools, cold hands and feet, dizziness on standing up and aversion to cold, the more closely they should avoid uncooked, chilled foods and drinks.

In addition, sugars and sweets directly damage the spleen. This is because sweet is the flavour which inherently 'gathers' in the spleen. It is also an inherently dampening flavour according to Chinese medicine. This means that the body engenders or secretes fluids which gather and collect, transforming into dampness, in response to foods with an excessively sweet flavour. In Chinese medicine, it is said that the spleen is averse to dampness. Dampness is yin and controls or checks yang qi. The spleen's function is based on the transformative and transporting functions of yang qi. Therefore, anything which is excessively dampening can damage the spleen. The sweeter a food is, the more dampening and, therefore, more damaging it is to the spleen.

Another group of foods which are dampening and, therefore, damaging to the spleen is what may be called 'sodden wheat foods'. This means flour products such as bread and noodles. Wheat (as opposed to rice) is damp by nature. When wheat is steamed, yeasted and/or refined, it becomes even more dampening. In addition, all oils and fats are damp by nature and, hence, may damage the spleen. The more oily or greasy a food is, the worse it is for the spleen. Because milk contains a lot of fat, dairy products are another spleen-damaging, dampness-engendering food. This includes milk, butter and cheese.

If we put this all together, then ice cream is just about the worst thing a person with a weak, damp spleen could eat. Ice cream is chilled, it is intensely sweet and it is filled with fat. Therefore, it is a triple whammy when it comes to damaging the spleen. Likewise, pasta smothered in tomato sauce and cheese is a recipe for disaster. Pasta made from wheat flour is dampening, as are both tomatoes and cheese. In addition, what many people don't realise is that a glass of fruit juice contains as much sugar as many sweets, and, therefore, is also very damaging to the spleen and damp-engendering.

Below is a list of specific Western foods which are either uncooked, chilled, too sweet or too dampening and thus damaging to the spleen. Persons with insomnia should minimise or avoid these according to how weak and damp their spleen is.

Ice cream	Biscuits and cakes
Sugar	Juicy, sweet fruits, such
Sweets, especially chocolate	as oranges, strawberries,
Milk	peaches and tomatoes
Butter	Fatty meats
Cheese	Fried foods
Margarine	Refined flour products
Yogurt	Yeasted bread
Raw salads	Nuts
Fruit juices	Alcohol (which is essentially
	sugar)

If the spleen is weak and wet, one should also not eat too much at any one time. A weak spleen can be overwhelmed by a large meal, especially if any of the food is hard to digest. This then results in food stagnation which only impedes the free flow of qi all the more and further damages the spleen.

A CLEAR, BLAND DIET

In Chinese medicine, the best diet for the spleen, and the body in general, is what is called a 'clear, bland diet'. This is a diet high in complex carbohydrates such as unrefined grains, especially rice and beans. It is a diet which is high in lightly cooked vegetables. It is a diet which is low in fatty meats, oily, greasy, fried foods and very sweet foods. However, it is not a completely vegetarian diet. I would recommend that most people eat one to two ounces of various types of meat two to four times per week. This animal flesh may be the highly popular chicken and fish, but should also include some lean beef, pork and lamb. Some fresh or cooked fruits may be eaten, but fruit juices should be avoided. In addition I would recommend that women make an effort to include tofu and tempeh, two soya products, in their diet.

If the spleen is weak, then one should eat several smaller meals rather than one or two large meals. In addition, because rice 1) is neutral in temperature, 2) fortifies the spleen and supplements the qi, and 3) eliminates dampness, rice should be the main or staple grain in the diet.

A FEW PROBLEM FOODS

Coffee

There are a few 'problem' foods which deserve special mention. The first of these is coffee. Many people crave coffee for two reasons. First, coffee moves stuck qi. Therefore, if a person suffers from liver depression qi stagnation, coffee will temporarily make them feel like their qi is flowing. Secondly, coffee transforms essence into qi and makes that qi temporarily available to the body. Therefore, people who suffer from spleen and/or kidney vacuity fatigue will get a temporary lift from coffee. They will feel like they have energy. However, once this energy is used up, they are left with a negative deficit. The coffee has transformed some of the essence stored in the kidneys into qi. This qi has been used, and now there is less stored essence. Since the blood and essence share a common source, coffee drinking may ultimately worsen insomnia associated with blood or kidney vacuities. Tea has a similar effect as coffee in that it transforms yin essence into yang qi and liberates that upwards and outwards through the body. However, the caffeine in black tea is usually only half as strong as in coffee.

Chocolate

Another problem food is chocolate. Chocolate is a combination of oil, sugar and cocoa. We have seen that both oil and sugar are dampening and damaging to the spleen. Temporarily, the sugar will boost the spleen qi, but ultimately it will result in 'sugar blues' or a hypoglycaemic let down. Cocoa stirs the life gate fire. The life gate fire is another name for kidney yang or kidney fire, and kidney fire is the source of sexual energy and desire. It is said that chocolate is the food of love, and from the Chinese medical point of view, that is true. Since chocolate stimulates kidney fire at the same time as it temporarily boosts the spleen, it does give one rush of yang qi. In addition, this rush of yang qi does move depression and stagnation, at least in the short-term. So it makes sense that some people with liver depression, spleen vacuity and kidney yang debility might crave chocolate.

Alcohol

Alcohol is both damp and hot according to Chinese medical theory. Hence, in English it is referred to as 'fire water'. It strongly moves the qi and blood. This means that people with liver depression qi stagnation will feel temporarily better after drinking alcohol. However, the sugar in alcohol damages the spleen and creates dampness which blocks the flow of energy. The heat (yang) in alcohol can damage the blood (yin) and aggrevate or inflame depressive liver heat. So, the end result is far from beneficial in most cases.

Hot, peppery foods

Spicy, peppery, 'hot' foods also move the qi, thereby giving some temporary relief to liver depression qi stagnation. However, like alcohol, the heat in spicy hot foods adversely affects the blood and can inflame yang.

Sour foods

In Chinese medicine, the sour flavour is inherently astringent and constricting. Therefore, people with liver depression qi stagnation should be careful not to use too much vinegar and other intensely sour foods. Such sour-flavoured foods will only aggravate the qi stagnation by restricting the qi and blood all the more. An excess of sweet and sour foods such as orange juice and tomatoes are not advised for people with liver depression and spleen vacuity. This is because the sour flavour constricts the qi whilst the sweet flavour damages the spleen and creates dampness.

Diet drinks

I have found in practice that diet drinks or sodas seem to contain something that damages the Chinese concept of the kidney energy. They may not damage the spleen in the same way that sugary drinks do, but that doesn't mean they are safe and healthy. I believe that diet drinks damage the kidney energies because a number of my patients over the years have reported that if they drink a lot of diet sodas, they experience urinary incontinence and soreness of the lower back and knees. When they stop drinking them these symptoms disappear. From the point of view of Chinese medical theory these are considered to be kidney vacuity symptoms. As women in their late 30s and throughout their 40s often have kidney vacuity signs I especially recommend that they steer clear of diet drinks. Anyone who has signs of kidney vacuity or weakness should avoid diet drinks, in my opinion. It is also interesting to note the recent reports on the connection between artificial sweeteners and cancer.

FOODS WHICH HELP NOURISH THE BLOOD

According to Chinese dietary therapy, all foods contain varying proportions of qi and *wei*. Qi means the ability to catalyse or promote yang function, while *wei* (literally meaning flavour) refers to a food's ability to nourish or construct yin substance. Since blood is relatively yin compared to qi being yang, a certain amount of food high in *wei* is necessary for a person to produce blood. Foods which are high in *wei* as compared to qi are those which tend to be heavy, dense, greasy or oily, meaty or bloody. All animal products contain more *wei* than vegetable products. At the same time, black beans or, even better, black soya beans contain more *wei* than celery or lettuce.

When people suffer from insomnia due to blood vacuity failing to nourish the heart and quiet the spirit or yin vacuity failing to control yang, they usually need to eat slightly more foods high in *wei*. This includes animal proteins and products, such as meat and eggs. It is said that flesh foods are very 'compassionate' to the human body. This word recognises the fact that the animal's life has had to be sacrificed to produce this type of food. It also recognises that, because such food is so close to the human body itself, it is especially nutritious. This means that for people who suffer from vacuity insomnia, eating some animal products is usually helpful and may sometimes even be necessary.

ANIMAL FOODS vs. VEGETARIANISM

Based on my many years of clinical experience, I have seen many Westerners who adhere to a strict vegetarian diet develop, after several years, blood or yin vacuity patterns. This is especially the case in women who lose blood every month and must build babies out of the blood and yin essence. When women who are strict vegetarians come to me with various complaints, if they present the signs and symptoms of blood vacuity, such as a swollen pale tongue, pale face, pale nails, pale lips, heart palpitations, insomnia and fatigue with a fine, forceless pulse, I usually recommend they they include a little animal food in their diet. They often report back to me how much better they feel for this change in diet and how much more energy they have.

The downside of eating meat – besides the ethical issues – are that foods which are high in *wei* also tend to be harder to digest and tend to engender phlegm and dampness. Therefore, such foods should only be eaten in very small amounts at any one time. In addition, the weaker the person's spleen or the more phlegm and dampness they already have, the less wet foods they should eat in order to get the correct balance. In addition, the weaker the person's spleen energy or the more phlegm and dampness they already have, the less *wei* foods they should eat in order to get the correct balance.

Remember above we said that the process of digestion first consisted of turning the food and drink ingested into 100°F soup in the stomach. Therefore, soups and broths made out of animal flesh are the easiest and most digestible way of adding some animal-quality *wei* to a person's diet. When eating flesh itself, this should probably be limited to only one to two ounces per serving and only three or four such servings per week. According to Chinese dietary theory, the best foods for creating and transforming blood and yin essence are organ meats and red or dark meats. This includes beef, venison, lamb and dark meat from chicken, turkey, goose and duck. White meat fish and white meat fowl are less effective for building blood. However, white meat pork is also fine, as is ham.

One good recipe for adding more digestible *wei* to the diet of a person who is blood vacuous is to take a marrow bone and boil this with some cut vegetables, especially root vegetables, and black beans or black soya beans. Such a marrow bone, black bean and vegetable soup is easy to digest and yet rich in *wei*.

THE PROVERBIAL GLASS OF HOT MILK

The fact that milk is rich in *wei* is exactly why it is a soporific or sleep-inducer according to Chinese medicine. Being high in *wei* or yin, milk helps control counterflowing, hyperactive yang. This is why drinking some warm milk before bed time is actually a good way to help insomnia *as long as the person does not suffer from either dampness or phlegm.* For persons with phlegm heat pattern insomnia, drinking a warm glass of milk before bed will typically make their insomnia worse. This is the beauty of Chinese medicine. The concepts allow one to determine on an individual basis whether any food, medicine, or activity will be good for a person's particular pattern of imbalance. The Chinese would say that blending a whole egg into boiling milk makes this time-tested remedy even more effective for enriching yin.

The most important thing to remember about diet is that if: A) the spleen is healthy and strong, B) one eats primarily a clear, bland diet with a little bit of animal food, C) one gets sufficient exercise, but D) one does not overtax oneself, then one will manufacture good amounts of qi and blood. Whatever of this qi and blood is left unconsumed at the end of the day will be transformed into acquired essence that night. This is the safest way of creating and transforming blood and yin via the diet. If one increases foods which are high in *wei*, these may supplement yin and nourish blood. Overloading, however, upsets the balance, and the net result will be less qi and blood not more, and the situation may be worsened as more phlegm and dampness have been created.

In the following chapter, the reader will find some specific recipes combining Chinese herbs and foods for nourishing the blood and enriching yin, quieting the spirit and promoting sleep.

SOME LAST WORDS ON DIET

In conclusion, Western patients are always asking me what they should eat in order to cure their disease. When it comes to diet, however, the issue is not so much what to eat as what not to eat. Diet most definitely plays a major role in the cause and perpetuation of many people's insomnia, but, except in the case of vegetarians suffering from blood or yin vacuities, the key issue is what to avoid or minimise, not what to eat. Most of us realise that coffee, chocolate, sugars and sweets, oils and fats, and alcohol are not good for us and that we should be eating more complex carbohydrates and freshly cooked vegetables and less fatty meats. Knowing what you ought to do is one thing and actually doing it is another.

To be perfectly honest, a clear, bland diet *à la* Chinese medicine is not the most exciting diet in the world. It is the traditional diet of our great-grandparents. Our modern Western diet, which is high in oils and fats, high in sugars and sweets, high in animal proteins, and proportionally high in uncooked, chilled foods and drinks, is a relatively recent development, and you can't fool Mother Nature.

When we change to the clear, bland diet of Chinese medicine we may at first suffer from cravings for more flavourful food. After a few days these cravings tend to disappear and we may be amazed that we don't miss some of our convenience or comfort foods as much as we thought we might. It is all too easy to become addicted to foods like sugar or caffeine which give us a short-term energy boost. Perseverance is the real key to long-term success. As the Chinese say, a million is made up of nothing but lots of ones, and a bucket is quickly filled by steady drips and drops.

EXERCISE

Exercise is the second of what I call the three free therapies. According to Chinese medicine, regular and adequate exercise has two basic benefits. First, exercise promotes the movement of the qi and quickening of the blood. Since almost all insomnia involves at least some component of liver depression qi stagnation, it is obvious that exercise is an important therapy for coursing the liver and rectifying the qi. Secondly, exercise benefits the spleen. The spleen's movement and transportation of the digestate is dependent upon the qi mechanism. The qi mechanism describes the function of the qi in bearing up the pure and bearing down the turbid parts of digestion. For the qi mechanism to function properly, the qi must be flowing normally and freely. Since exercise moves and rectifies the qi, it also helps regulate and rectify the qi mechanism. This then results in the spleen's movement and transportation of foods and liquids and its subsequent creating and transforming of the qi and blood. As spleen and qi and blood vacuity typically complicate most people's insomnia and because a healthy spleen checks and controls a depressed liver, exercise treats one of the other commonly encountered disease mechanisms in the majority of Westerners suffering from insomnia. Regular, adequate exercise is thus a vitally important component of any person's regime for either preventing or treating insomnia.

WHAT KIND OF EXERCISE IS
BEST FOR INSOMNIA?

Aerobics

In my experience, I find aerobic exercise to be the most beneficial for most people with insomnia. By aerobic exercise, I mean _any physical activity which raises one's heart beat 80% above one's normal resting rate and keeps it there for at least 20 minutes._ To calculate your normal resting heart rate, place your fingers over the pulsing artery on the front side of your neck. Count the beats for 15 seconds and then multiply by four. This gives you your beats per minute or BPM. Now multiply your BPM by 0.8. Take the resulting number and add it to your resting BPM. This gives you your aerobic threshold of BPM. Next engage in any physical activity you like. After you have been exercising for five minutes, take your pulse for 15 seconds once again at the artery on the front side of your throat. Multiply the resulting count by four and this tells you your current BPM. If this number is less than your aerobic threshold BPM, then you know you need to exercise harder or faster. Once you get your heart rate up to your aerobic threshold, then you need to keep exercising at the same level of intensity for at least 20 minutes. In order to ensure that you are keeping your heart beat high enough for long enough, you should recount your pulse every five minutes or so.

Depending on your age and physical condition, the amount of exercise you require to reach your aerobic threshold will vary. For some, simply walking briskly will raise the heartbeat 80% above its resting rate. Others will need to do running, swimming, cycling or some other more strenuous form of exercise. It really does not matter what the exercise is as long as it raises your heart beat 80% above your resting rate and keeps it there for 20 minutes. There are two other criteria that you may wish to consider. Firstly, the exercise should be something that is not too boring. If it is too boring, then you may have a hard time keeping it up. Secondly, the type of exercise should not cause any damage to any parts of the body. For instance, running on pavements may cause knee problems for some people. Therefore, you should pick a type of exercise you enjoy but also one which will not cause any problems.

When doing aerobic exercise, it is best to exercise either every day or every other day. If you do not do your aerobics at least once every 72 hours, then its cumulative effects will not be as great. I recommend to my patients with insomnia that they do some sort of aerobic exercises every day or every other day, three to four times per week *at least*. The good news is that there is no real need to exercise more than 30 minutes at any one time. Forty-five minutes per session is not going to be all that much better than 25 minutes per session. And 25 minutes four times per week is very much better than one hour once a week.

Weight training

Recent research has also demonstrated that weight lifting can help relieve depression in women of all ages.[16] Insomnia is one of the important symptoms of depression. I have now begun to recommend lifting weights on the days when you are not doing aerobics. In general, you should not lift weights every day unless you vary the muscle groups you are working each day. In the study on weight lifting and depression cited above, the women lifted weights which were 45–87% as heavy as the maximum they could lift at one time. Those women who lifted weights closer to the top end of this range saw the greatest benefits. These women lifted weights three days per week for 10 weeks, gradually increasing the amount of weight they lifted at each session.

---

[16] 'Depression and Weight Training', *Harvard Women's Health Watch*, Vol. IV, No.6, February 1997, reporting on research published in the *Journal of Gerontology*, January 1997.

As weight lifting requires some initial training and education in order to do it safely and properly, I recommend taking classes either at a local gym, recreation centre or from a personal fitness trainer. When aerobics are alternated with weight lifting, you have a really comprehensive training regime designed to benefit both your cardiovascular system and muscles, tendons, ligaments and bones. Regular weight-bearing exercise is also important for preventing osteoporosis.

TOO MUCH EXERCISE

While the vast majority of people with insomnia will benefit from more exercise, there are a few who actually need less physical activity. As we have seen, all stirring or activity entails a consumption of yin by yang. If an individual is either constitutionally yin vacuous or, due to some circumstance, like ageing, enduring disease, extreme blood loss, excessive births or lactation, has become yin vacuous, then too much exercise or physical activity can worsen that yin vacuity. This is mostly seen in women with thin bodily constitutions who overexercise, such as professional athletes, or in women who suffer from anorexia and bulimia.

Body fat in Chinese medicine is considered to be yin. Therefore, people who are very thinly built tend to have less yin to begin with. If, through exercise, they reduce their body fat even more, they may become so deficient in yin that it can no longer control yang. In some women, an insufficiency of yin blood due to too much exercise usually manifests itself first as cessation of menstruation, or amenorrheoa. It is also possible for drug use, especially types of 'speed', or anorexia and bulimia to result in an overconsumption of yin leading to amenorrhoea on the one hand and increased mental agitation and insomnia on the other. Here I am using the term bulimia to mean binging and purging, i.e., eating but vomiting back up whatever has been ingested. Although the woman may be eating, she may not be getting sufficient yin nourishment.

For some women, it may be necessary to decrease the amount of exercise they are getting. If the amount of exercise you do is balanced you will feel refreshed and invigorated a couple of hours after you have finished exercising. If on the other hand, you feel even more fatigued or even nervous and jittery then you are probably doing too much and should consider cutting down.

DEEP RELAXATION

As we have seen above, insomnia is commonly associated with liver depression qi stagnation. If liver depression endures or is severe, it typically transforms into heat or fire. Heat or fire, being yang, consume and exhaust yin and blood. Thus yang qi moves frenetically upwards, disturbing the heart spirit. Therefore, liver depression is often at the root of insomnia. In Chinese medicine liver depression comes from feelings of frustration. This then creates emotional depression and easy anger or irritability. According to Chinese medicine the emotion of anger results in the qi ascending or moving upwards.

When we feel frustrated, stressed or angry about something, we often tense our muscles. We especially tense the muscles of the upper back, neck and shoulders and may also hold our breath in at the same time. This action of tensing and holding the breath has the effect of constricting the flow of qi. This then leads to further liver depression and qi stagnation. In order to break this cycle we need to relax and cope better with life's frustrations.

Deep relaxation is, therefore, the third of the three free therapies. For deep relaxation to be therapeutic medically, it needs to be more than just mental equilibrium. It needs to be somatic or bodily relaxation as well as mental repose. In Chinese medicine, *every emotion is associated with a change in the direction or flow of qi*: for example, anger makes the qi move upwards; fear, on the other hand, makes the qi move downwards. Anger makes us feel as if we could blow our top or explode with anger. Fear may cause a sinking feeling, we feel paralysed or frozen with fear. All emotions are not just mental but bodily or somatic events. This is why it is important to clear your mind and relax your body at the same time.

GUIDED DEEP RELAXATION TAPES

One of the most effective ways I have found for both myself and my patients to practise deep mental and physical relaxation is to use a guided progressive relaxation tape on a daily basis. Such tapes have a narrator who leads you through the process of relaxation, allowing you to relax each part of the body progressively. There are many such tapes available these days through specialist shops. I recommend that you choose one or two that you feel comfortable with and enjoy listening to. In this way if you get bored of one you can go onto another.

HOW TO CHOOSE A GOOD RELAXATION TAPE

There are four key things to look for to maximise the therapeutic effect of a good relaxation tape. First I would recommend that you ensure the tape is a guided tape and not a subliminal relaxation tape. Subliminal tapes usually have music, and any instructions to relax are given so quietly that they are not consciously heard. Although such tapes can help you feel relaxed when you do them, ultimately they do not teach you how to relax as a skill which can be consciously practised and refined. Secondly, make sure the tape starts from the top of the body and works downwards. Remember, anger makes the qi go upwards in the body, and people with irritability and easy anger due to liver depression qi stagnation already have too much qi rising upwards in their bodies. Such depressed qi typically needs to be moved downwards. Thirdly, make sure the tape instructs you to relax your physical body. If you do not relax all your muscles or sinews, the qi cannot flow freely and the liver cannot be coursed. Depression is not resolved, and there will not be the same medically therapeutic effect. And finally choose a tape which instructs you to let your breath go with each exhalation. One of the symptoms of liver depression is a stuffy feeling in the chest which we then unconsciously try to relieve by sighing. Letting each exhalation go completely helps the lungs to push the qi downwards. This allows the lungs to control the liver at the same time as it bears down upwardly counterflowing angry liver qi.

CALMING EXERCISE AND MEDITATION

More and more people these days are recognising the need to introduce some form of calming exercise or meditation into their life in order to cope better with stress. There are so many things now available for you to try, here are a few suggestions:

Yoga

T'ai Chi

Qi Gong

Aikido and some
  martial arts

Meditation (whilst this can be a spiritual practice it can also provide an enormously beneficial and calming effect on the emotions)

THE IMPORTANCE OF DAILY RELAXATION

When I was an intern in Shanghai in the People's Republic of China, I was once taken on a field trip to a hospital clinic where they were using deep relaxation as a therapy with patients with high blood pressure, heart disease, stroke, migraines and insomnia. The doctors at this clinic showed us various graphs plotting their research data on how such daily, progressive deep relaxation can regulate the blood pressure and body temperature and improve the appetite, digestion, elimination, sleep, energy and mood. One of the things they said has stuck with me for 15 years: 'Small results in 100 days, big results in 1,000.' This means that if one does such daily, progressive deep relaxation *every single day for 100 days*, one will definitely experience certain results. What are these 'small' results? These small results are improvements in all the parameters listed above: blood pressure, body temperature, appetite, digestion, elimination, sleep, energy and mood. If these are 'small' results, then what are the 'big' results experienced in 1,000 days of practice? The 'big' results are a change in how one reacts to stress – in other words, a change in one's very personality or character.

What these doctors in Shanghai stressed and what I have also experienced both personally and with my patients is that it is vitally important to do such daily, guided, progressive deep relaxation every single day, day in and day out for a solid three months at least and for a continuous three years at best. If one does such progressive, somatic deep relaxation every day, *one will see every parameter or measurement of health and well-being improve*. If one does this kind of deep relaxation only sporadically, missing a day here and there, it will feel good when you do it, but it will not have the marked, cumulative therapeutic effects that it could have. Perseverance is the real key to getting the benefits of deep relaxation.

THE REAL TEST

Having a daily relaxation practice is really important but it's not the real goal. The ultimate goal is to learn how to deal with stress more effectively, breathing out and relaxing your body rather than holding your breath and tensing up. By doing such deep relaxation every day you will gradually learn how to re-condition your body to stress. This is the real test, the game of life!

FINDING THE TIME

If you're like me and most of my patients, you are probably asking yourself right now, 'All this is well and good, but when am I supposed to find the time to eat well-balanced cooked meals, exercise at least every other day, and do a deep relaxation every day? I'm already stretched to the breaking point.' I know. That's the problem.

As a clinician, I often wish I could wave a magic wand over my patients' heads and make them all healthy and well. I cannot. After close to two decades of working with thousands of patients, I know of no easy way to health. There is good living and there is easy living. What most people take as the easy way these days is to continue pushing their limits continually to the maximum. The so-called path of least resistance is actually the path of plentiful resistance. Unless you take time for yourself and find the time to eat well, exercise and relax, no treatment is going to eliminate your insomnia completely. There is simply no pill you can pop or food you can eat that will get rid of the root causes of insomnia: poor diet, too little exercise and too much stress. Even Chinese herbal medicine and acupuncture can only get their full effect if diet and lifestyle are first adjusted. Sun Si-maio, the most famous Chinese doctor of the Tang dynasty (618–907 CE), who himself refused government office and lived to be 101, said: 'First adjust the diet and lifestyle and only secondarily give herbs and acupuncture.' Likewise, it is said today in China, 'Three parts treatment, seven parts nursing.' This means that any cure is only 30% due to medical treatment and 70% is due to nursing, meaning proper diet and lifestyle.

In my experience, this is absolutely true. Seventy per cent of all disease will improve after three months of proper diet, exercise, relaxation and lifestyle modification. Seventy per cent! Each of us has certain non-discretionary rituals we perform each day. For instance, you may always and without exception find the time to brush your teeth. Perhaps it is always finding the time to shower. For others, it may be always finding the time each day to eat lunch. And for the vast majority of us, we find the time to get dressed every day. The same applies to good eating, exercise and deep relaxation. Where there's a will there's a way. If your insomnia is bad enough, you can find the time to eat well, get proper exercise and do a daily deep relaxation tape.

When it comes to daily deep relaxation and insomnia, the good news is that the right time is just before bed. Therefore, you do not have to find some other time to do this in the middle of your busy day. When you lie down at night, turn on your guided, progressive deep relaxation tape. You might even find that you have fallen asleep before the tape is finished.

THE SOLUTION TO INSOMNIA IS IN YOUR HANDS

In Boulder, Colorado where I live, we have a pedestrian area in the centre of town. On summer evenings, my wife and I often walk through it. Having treated so many patients over the years, it is not unusual for me to meet former patients on these strolls. Frequently when we say hello, these patients begin by telling me they are sorry they haven't been in to see me in such a long time. They usually apologise. I then usually ask if they've been all right. Often they say: 'When my problem flares up, I remember what you told me about my diet, exercise and lifestyle. I then go back to doing my exercise or deep relaxation or I change my diet, and then my symptoms go away. That's why I haven't been in. I'm sorry.'

This type of story is music to my ears. When I hear that these patients are now able to control their own conditions by following the dietary and lifestyle advice I gave them, I know that, as a Chinese doctor, I have done my job correctly. In Chinese medicine, it is said the inferior doctor treats disease after it has appeared. The superior doctor prevents disease before it has arisen. If I can teach my patients how to cure their symptoms themselves by making changes in their diet and lifestyle, then I know I'm really doing the best I can for them.

To get the real benefits of Chinese medicine, it is vital to make the necessary changes to diet and lifestyle. Insomnia is not an illness that is cured once and forever like measles or mumps. When I say Chinese medicine can cure insomnia, I do not mean that you will never experience unwanted wakefulness again. What I mean is that Chinese medicine can eliminate or greatly reduce your symptoms *as long as you keep your diet and lifestyle together.* As a Chinese Medicine Practitioner I try to give my patients an understanding of what causes their disease and what they can do to minimise or eliminate its causes and mechanisms. It is then up to them to decide what is an acceptable level of health.

SIMPLE HOME REMEDIES
FOR INSOMNIA

As we have seen diet, exercise and relaxation may all play an important role in helping with insomnia. We will now look at a number of simple remedies which may be done at home to help with this condition.

REGULATING SLEEP AND WAKE CYCLES

It is very common for someone who has had trouble either falling asleep or staying asleep to lay in bed in the morning in an effort to make up the sleep they lost at night. This creates havoc with the sleep cycles. If you sleep later in the day to make up the sleep you lost the night before, you will only further set your sleep–wake cycle back. Instead of feeling sleepy at your normal bedtime, you will naturally stay awake later into the evening.

I generally advise my insomniac patients not to lie in bed past their normal rising time in the morning. Yes, one probably will feel tired sooner in the day because of the lost sleep, but this is exactly what the doctor ordered – well, wanted. It is also best, if possible, not to nap during the day if you are having trouble sleeping at night. This will likewise tend to reset your sleep–wake cycle in a negative way. If you are able to go to sleep at the right time at night without difficulty, then a little nap is no problem. If you suffer from insomnia, it is best not to nap and not to lie in bed in the mornings.

CHINESE AROMATHERAPY

In Chinese medicine, the qi is seen as a type of wind or vapour. The Chinese character for qi shows wind blowing over a rice field. In addition, smells are often referred to as a thing's qi.

Therefore, there is a close relationship between smells carried through the air and the flow of qi in a person's body. Although aromatherapy has not been a major part of professionally practised Chinese medicine for almost a thousand years, there is a simple aromatherapy treatment which you can do at home that can help alleviate pre-menstrual irritability, depression, nervousness, anxiety and insomnia.

In Chinese, *Chen Xiang* means 'sinking fragrance'. It is the name of Lignum Aquilariae Agallochae or Eaglewood. This is a frequent ingredient in Asian incense formulas. In Chinese medicine, Aquilaria is classified as a qi-rectifying medicinal. When used as a boiled decoction or 'tea', Aquilaria moves the qi and stops pain, bears down upward counterflow and regulates the middle (i.e., the spleen and stomach), and promotes the kidneys' grasping of the qi sent down by the lungs. I believe that the word sinking in this herb's name refers to this medicinal's effect on upward counterflowing qi. Eventually upward counterflowing qi must accumulate in the heart, disturbing and causing restlessness of the heart spirit. When this medicinal wood is burnt and its smoke is inhaled as a medicinal incense, its sinking and spirit-calming function is emphasised.

You can buy Aquilaria or *Chen Xiang* from Chinese herb shops or suppliers. It is best to use the powdered variety. However, powder may be made by putting a small piece of this aromatic wood in a coffee grinder. It is fine to use small bits of the wood if powder is not available. You will also need to buy a roll of incense charcoals. Place a charcoal in a non-flammable dish and light it with a match. Then sprinkle a few pinches of Aquilaria powder on the lit charcoal. As the smoke rises, breathe in deeply. This can be done on a regular basis one or more times per day during the pre-menstruum or on an as-needed basis if you suffer from restlessness, nervousness, anxiety, irritability or depression. If you suffer from insomnia, you can carry out this 'treatment' when lying in bed at night.

Chinese aromatherapy with Lignum Aquilariae Agallochae is very cheap and effective. And as far as I know it has no side effects or contra-indications.

HYDROTHERAPY

Hydrotherapy means water therapy and is also a feature of traditional Chinese medicine. There are several different water treatments for helping relieve insomnia. First, let's begin with a warm bath. If you take a warm bath (90–95°F) for 15–20 minutes, it can free and smooth the flow of qi and blood. It may also calm the spirit and hasten sleep. Taking a warm bath half an hour before going to bed can help insomnia. It is even more effective to put a cloth soaked in cold water on the forehead whilst taking the bath.

It is important, when using a warm bath, not to use water so hot or to lie in the bath for so long that sweat breaks out on your forehead. Because 'fluids and blood share a common source', excessive sweating can cause problems for women with blood and yin vacuities. Therefore, unless you are given a specific hot bath prescription by your Chinese Medical Practitioner, I suggest people suffering from insomnia do not stay in warm baths until they sweat. They may feel pleasantly relaxed at the time but may later feel excessively fatigued or hot and thirsty. The latter is particularly important for women who are peri-menopausal. For these women, hot baths may increase hot flushes and night sweats.

If the cause of the insomnia is depression transforming heat, yang qi is exuberant and counterflowing upwards. Other symptoms might be migraines, tension headaches, hot flushes, night sweats, painful, red eyes, or even nosebleeds. For this case, you can tread in cold water up to your ankles for 15–20 minutes at a time. A variation of this is to fill one bucket with hot water (115°F) and another bucket with cold (60°F). First, place both feet in the hot water for three minutes, and then place them in the cold water for 30 seconds. Repeat this procedure four times for each treatment. Afterwards, dry your feet, put on warm socks, and go to bed. Another method is to soak heavy socks in cold water and then put them on before going to bed. Wrap them in plastic or a thick towel and remain in bed warmly covered. The last hydrotherapy method is to soak a towel in cold water and use this as a compress on the abdomen, cover it with a plastic sheet or thick towel. All these treatments aim to draw yang qi away from the head to the lower part of the body. As we have a cold damp climate in the UK, I recommend the use of cold compresses with caution, particularly if your lower abdomen feels cold to the touch. If you feel the cold easily then the use of cold compresses may not be appropriate for you.

CHINESE SELF-MASSAGE

Massage, including self-massage, is a highly developed part of Traditional Chinese Medicine. The self-massage regime below is specifically designed as a home remedy for insomnia.

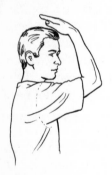

Begin by pressing and kneading the very centre and top of the skull. This is acupoint *Bai Hui* (GV 20). It is the most yang point in the body, the meeting place of all the yang channels and vessels. It is especially useful for calming the spirit, soothing the liver, and subduing hyperactive yang. Do this about 100 times.

Next, knead with the fingertips of both hands the acupoint located at the inner ends of the eyebrows. This area corresponds to the point _Zhan Zhu_ (Bl 2). It is the place where the yang qi travelling up the _yang qiao mai_ connects with the _yin qiao mai_ which leads downwards. Knead this area approximately 30 times.

Third, with the index fingers and thumbs, wipe the upper edge of the eye bone and then the lower edge. Work from the inner corners of the eyes to the outer corners. This helps to move the yang qi in the eyes downwards and stops it from congesting in the _yang qiao mai_ in the eyes. Do this 20–30 times.

Fourth, rub the palms of the hands vigorously together until they feel warm. Then place these warm palms over both eyes. Cover the eyes thus for 30–60 seconds and then lightly rub the closed eyes approximately 10 times.

Fifth, press and knead the acupoint _Feng Chi_ (GB 20) with the thumbs. This point is located in the depression between the mastoid process, the bone behind the ear, and the strap muscles on either side of the spine, which connect at the base of the skull. The point is located approximately one inch within

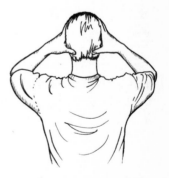

the hairline on most people. It is a point most people instinctively massage when they have a tension headache or stiff neck. Do this 30–50 times, massaging both points with both hands at the same time.

Sixth, rub circles around the centre of the upper and then lower abdomen. The point in the middle of the upper abdomen is called *Zhong Wan* (CV 12). The point in the centre of the lower abdomen is called *Guan Yuan* (CV 4). Rub these first clockwise and then counterclockwise approximately 100 times each point in each direction.

Seventh, press and knead the acupoint *Nei Guan* (Per 6). This point is located on the inner side of the forearm in between the two tendons. It is located about 4cm/1½in upwards from the wrist. First press and knead with the thumb of one hand, and

 then press and knead with the thumb of the other. Do this approximately 30–50 times on each side. This point helps soothe the liver, regulate the qi and quiet the spirit.

 Eighth, press and knead the point *Shen Men* (Ht 7). This is located on the inner side of the forearm at the crease of the wrist right below the base of the little finger. Massage the

points on both wrists 30–50 times each. This point clears heat from the heart and quiets the spirit.

Now, press and knead the point *Zu San Li* (St 36). This point is located three inches below the lower, outside edge of the kneecap when the leg is bent. It is located in a depression between the muscles of the lower leg. Massage this point 30–50 times on each side. This point regulates the qi and leads upwardly counterflowing yang qi downwards.

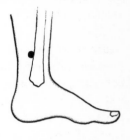

Follow this by pressing and kneading *San Yin Jiao* (Sp 6). This point is located three inches above the tip of the inner anklebone on the back side of the lower leg bone. It is the meeting place of the liver, spleen and kidney channels. It is a very effective way of stimulating the production of yin blood in the body which can then 'magnetise' yang qi back downwards.

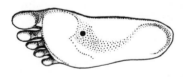

And lastly, rub the depression just behind and to the side of the ball of the foot. This point is called *Yong Quan* (Ki 1). If *Bai Hui* (GV 20) is the most yang point in the body, *Yong Quan* is the most yin.

Stimulating this point helps to lead counterflowing yang qi back downwards to its lower source. Rub this point with the palm of the opposite hand until it feels hot. Repeat this on the other foot.

This self-massage regime should take approximately 20 minutes to half an hour. It should be done every evening just before bed. When doing each massage manipulation, it is best to try and calmly focus on the physical sensations under your hands and not let your mind wander to your day's worries and stresses.

TOPICAL APPLICATION OF CHINESE MEDICINALS

A safe and simple way of stimulating the healing properties of the acupuncture points is to apply Chinese medicinals to them. *Here are two remedies:*

Grind 9g of Fructus Evodiae Rutecarpae (*Wu Zhu Yu*) into a powder and mix it into a paste with rice vinegar. Apply this paste over the point *Yong Quan* (Ki 1), described in the above Chinese self-massage protocol, on both feet. Cover with an adhesive plaster. Do this before bed each night, and then remove and wash off the paste in the morning.

Another medicinal paste for topical application on *Yong Quan* (Ki 1) in the same way as described above is to powder some Fructus Evodiae Rutecarpae (*Wu Zhu Yu*) and Cortex Cinnamomi Cassiae (*Rou Gui*). Mix this powder with a little warm alcohol to make a paste and apply as above.

SEVEN STAR HAMMERING

A seven star hammer is a small hammer or mallet with seven small needles embedded in its head. Nowadays in China, it is often called a skin or dermal needle. It is one of the ways that a person can stimulate various acupuncture points without actually inserting a needle into the body. Seven star hammers can be used either for people who are frightened of needles, for children, or for home therapy. When the points to be stimulated are on the front of the body, you can carry out this technique for yourself. If the points are located on the back of the body, then you will need to ask a family member or friend to help. This is a very easy technique and does not require any special training or expertise.

At least part of the seven star treatment for insomnia will require a helper. First, disinfect all the areas of the skin which are going to be tapped. Then begin by lightly tapping on the back of the neck. One should lightly tap all along the centre of the spine on the neck as well as up and down the strap muscles to either side of the spinal column. Then lightly tap the point _Feng Chi_ (GB 20) bilaterally. The location of this point behind the ear mastoid processes at the base of the skull has been described in the section on Chinese self-massage above. If you suffer from ascendant hyperactivity of liver yang, you can tap till the points bleed slightly. This helps drain heat or fire from the upper body. Otherwise tap until the skin is simply flushed red.

Next, tap all over the sacrum lightly until it turns a light red colour. This is the triangular-shaped bone at the base of the spine.

Follow this by tapping _Nei Guan_ (Per 6), _Shen Men_ (Ht 7), and _San Yin Jiao_ (Sp 6) in that order. The locations of these three points have also been given under the section on Chinese self-massage above.

If there is headache due to ascendant hyperactivity of liver yang, tap over both temples. If the headache is severe, tap till just a little blood is let.

If there is any bleeding, wipe the area with a cotton swab moistened in alcohol or hydrogen peroxide. Then take a dry cotton ball and press the area. Between treatments, soak the seven star hammer in alcohol or hydrogen peroxide and never share hammers between people so as to prevent infection. Seven star hammers are inexpensive. They may be purchased from Chinese medical suppliers, which are listed in a later section.

CHINESE HERBAL REMEDIES FOR HOME THERAPY

In this next section I will give some recipes which you can make at home in the form of wines, porridges and teas. As with all Chinese herbs I strongly recommend that you seek professional guidance with regard to their usage. You may find that you have difficulties getting hold of the ingredients, as herbal suppliers in the UK do not sell directly to the public. Should you choose to try one of these recipes and notice any adverse side-effects, stop taking it immediately and seek professional advice.

CHINESE MEDICINAL WINES

Chinese medicinal wines are part of Chinese dietary therapy. They make use of alcohol's special characteristics as well as a few Chinese herbs or medicinals. Although alcohol is hot and can inflame yang heat, especially liver heat, it has the effect of moving depressed qi and static blood. It also speeds and increases the medicinal effects of herbs into and in the body.

If there is liver–blood–kidney yin vacuity, then the treatment principles are to supplement the kidneys and nourish the liver. This can be done by soaking 150g/5oz of Fructus Lycii Chinensis (*Gou Qi Zi*) in 1 litre/1¾pts of brandy for 1–2 months. After the herbs have soaked, remove the dregs and then take 30–45ml/2–3tbsp each night before bed. Another possibility is to soak 150g/5oz of Radix Polygoni Multiflori in 900ml/2pts of brandy for a couple of months. Later, remove the dregs, and take

30–45ml/2–3tbsp before or after dinner. Do not use this Chinese medicinal wine if there is diarrhoea or chronically loose stools.

For heart–blood–spleen qi vacuity insomnia, you can try either of two self-made Chinese medicinal wines. The first is made by placing 150g/5oz of white Ginseng (Radix Panacis Ginseng, *Ren Shen*) in 1 litre/1¾pts of brandy for 1–2 months. Remove the dregs, and take 30–45ml/2–3tbsp before or after dinner. Do not use this wine if you display the symptoms of ascendant hyperactivity of liver yang. You could also use 150g/5oz of Arillus Euphoriae Longanae (*Long Yan Rou*) steeped in 900ml/2pts of sake. In this case, drink 30–45ml/2–3tbsp before or after dinner each evening. Do not take this medicinal wine if you suffer from constipation.

For insomnia due to phlegm blocking the orifices of the heart, take 120g/4½oz of Rhizoma Acori Graminei (*Shi Chang Pu*) and soak this in 1 litre/1¾pts of vodka for 3–5 days. Then take 10–20ml/2–4tsp of the resulting medicinal wine three times per day on an empty stomach.

CHINESE MEDICINAL PORRIDGES

Like the Chinese medicinal wines discussed above, Chinese medicinal porridges are a specialised part of Chinese dietary therapy. Because porridges are already in the form of 100°F soup, they are a particularly good way of eating nutritious but nevertheless hard-to-digest grains. When Chinese medicinals are cooked along with those grains, one has a high-powered but easily assimilated 'health food' of the first order.

For yin vacuity insomnia, boil 60g/2½oz of Bulbus Lilii (*Bai He*) along with 100g/4oz of white rice. Add a little brown sugar to taste and eat once each day for 10 days. Another medicinal porridge for treating yin vacuity insomnia can be made by first boiling 50g/2oz of uncooked Radix Rehmanniae (*Sheng Di*) and 50g/2oz of Semen Zizyphi Spinosae (*Suan Zao Ren*) into a 'tea' for 30–45 minutes. Then use this 'tea' to boil 100g/4oz of white rice into a gruel. Eat this as often as you like on a daily basis.

For heart–blood–spleen qi vacuity insomnia, cook 100g/4oz of white rice with 50g/2oz of Semen Coicis Lachryma-jobi (*Yi Yi Ren*) and 10 red dates (Fructus Zizyphi Jujubae, *Da Zao*). Eat this once a day. Another recipe is to cook 50g/2oz of Sclerotium Poriae Cocos (*Fu Ling*) with 100g/4oz of white rice using enough water to make a thin porridge or gruel.

CHINESE MEDICINAL TEAS

Chinese medicinal teas may be seen as either Chinese herbal medicine or as Chinese dietary therapy. They consist of using only one or two Chinese herbal medicinals in order to make a tea which is then drunk throughout the day. Such Chinese medicinal teas are usually easier to make and taste better than multi-ingredient, professionally prescribed decoctions. They can be used as an adjunct to other Chinese therapies for insomnia.

For yin and blood vacuity insomnia, grind 15g/½oz of Semen Biotae Orientalis (*Bai Zi Ren*) into pieces. Boil with water and add honey to taste. Drink either before or after dinner. Or boil 15g/½oz of Fructus Mori Albi (*Sang Shen*) in water. Remove the dregs and drink one packet per day.

For phlegm obstruction with liver yang hyperactivity, i.e., gallbladder timidity, grind Rhizoma Acori Graminei (*Shi Chang Pu*), 6g/1tsp, Flos Jasmini (*Mo Li Hua*), 6g/1tsp, and green tea, 10g/1¾tsp, into coarse powder. Soak some of this powder in boiling water and drink as a tea any time of the day. The doses given are for one day's supply. Another formula for gallbladder timidity consists of Dens Draconis (*Long Chi*), 10g/1¾tsp, and Rhizoma Acori Graminei (*Shi Chang Pu*), 3g/½tsp. First boil the Dens Draconis in water for 10 minutes. Then add the Rhizoma Acori Graminei and continue boiling for another 10–15 minutes. Remove the dregs and drink any time of the day, 1–2 packets per day.

For fire disturbing the heart spirit, boil 60g/2oz each of Medulla Junci Effusi (*Deng Xin Cao*) and Folium Lophatheri Gracilis (*Dan Zhu Ye*). Remove the dregs and drink the resulting tea warm at any time of the day, one packet per day.

FLOWER THERAPY

The beauty of flowers is a wonderful way to bring joy into your life. Joy is so important because it is such a healing emotion. This is very good for insomnia where emotional turmoil may be present.

As well as the beauty of flowers there is also their smell. Chrysanthemums, for example, have a relaxing and calming aroma. The smell of roses is said to quicken the blood in Chinese medicine. Flowers which are used to calm the spirit and relieve stress in Chinese herbal medicine are: lily, narcissus, lotus, orchids and jasmine. Taking a good sniff of a bouquet of flowers is a great way to release pent-up tensions.

CREATING A PERSONAL REGIME

I have given you a selection of home treatments in this chapter to help with insomnia. It is up to you how you might combine and use the treatments: there really are no hard and fast rules. Try what appeals to you most. If your symptoms are very severe then you may wish to use two or three treatments at one time although it is difficult to see the benefits if you are doing too many things at once. Have fun!

KICKING THE SEDATIVE HABIT

Some readers may be currently using Western sleep medications, either over-the-counter medications or prescription sedatives and 'tranquillisers'. In general, it is not a good idea to discontinue such medications abruptly without checking with your Western physician. Your Western physician will be able to tell you whether or not you can stop taking a medication immediately or whether it needs to be tapered off using a certain schedule.

It is best if your GP and your Chinese Medical Practitioner can work hand in hand. Therefore, if you are currently taking any Western medication, whether prescription or over-the-counter, it is important to tell your Chinese medical practitioner what you are taking. In general, there is no problem with taking Western sedatives and tranquillisers with Chinese medicinals, or at the same time as receiving acupuncture for insomnia. If anything, the Chinese medical treatment will make the Western medicines work better and with less side effects. What you should notice fairly quickly is that you need to take less and less of your Western medications to achieve the same or even better ability to go and stay asleep. Thus acupuncture and Chinese medicinals can actually help you to get off Western sedatives and tranquillisers at the same time as addressing the root of your insomnia.

In particular, ear acupuncture has been used extensively both in Britain and the USA to help people deal with drug and alcohol addictions. Press needles can be embedded in the ear between treatments; this technique allows the calming therapy of acupuncture to exert a continuous effect. By using this method of ear acupuncture, one may lessen any withdrawal symptoms and nervousness when reducing or stopping Western sedatives and tranquillisers.

Anyone who suffers from mental disorders, such as schizophrenia or bi-polar disorder (*aka* manic depression), *should not stop taking their Western medication.* Acupuncture and Chinese medicine may help relieve any side-effects from such Western medication, but are typically not sufficient taken alone. Anyone suffering from severe depression with any thoughts of suicide should immediately seek help from a qualified Western physician or psychotherapist.

In general I strongly recommend that you seek the advice and support of your doctor should you wish to reduce or stop taking medication.

CHINESE MEDICAL RESEARCH
ON INSOMNIA

his chapter will focus on recent research articles published in Chinese medical journals that relate to insomnia. This type of research is outcome-based and more of a clinical audit than a strict clinical trial. In my opinion, it is difficult, and perhaps not appropriate, to assess traditional medicines (which have been tried and tested over thousands of years) by exactly the same methods as modern pharmaceuticals might be assessed.

These outcome-based clinical audits are often much closer to a real-life situation and they measure patient satisfaction. I hope that the research articles I have presented here offer some very convincing and persuasive examples of how Chinese medicine has helped with the treatment of insomnia.

'The Treatment of 22 Cases of Insomnia in Young Adults Mainly by Acupuncturing *Si Shen Cong* (M-HN-1)' by Piao Ming-hua, *Hei Long Jiang Zhong Yi Yao* (*Heilongjiang Chinese Medicine and Medicinals*), 1995, No. 6, pp. 38–39

All 22 patients in this clinical audit were seen as outpatients. There were 12 females and 10 males. The youngest was 11 years old and the oldest was 28. The shortest course of disease was seven days and the longest was four years. Eighteen cases had already been administered Western sedatives. Either these had not produced a markedly good effect or they had caused side effects. The author mentions that insomnia in young adults is mostly due to overtaxation and thinking too much.

The treatment method mainly consisted of needling *Si Shen Cong* (M-HN-1). If there was heart–spleen detriment and decline, *Xin Shu* (Bl 15), *Pi Shu* (Bl 20), and *Jue Yin Shu* (Bl 14) were added. If heart and kidneys were not interacting, *Xin Shu*

(Bl 15), *Shen Shu* (Bl 23), and *Tai Xi* (Ki 3) were added. If there was heart–gallbladder vacuity and timidity, *Xin Shu* (Bl 15), *Dan Shu* (Bl 19), and *Da Ling* (Per 7) were added. If there was spleen-stomach disharmony, *Wei Shu* (Bl 21) and *Zu San Li* (St 36) were added. And if there was ascendant hyperactivity of liver yang, *Gan Shu* (Bl 18), *Jian Shi* (Per 5), and *Tai Chong* (Liv 3) were added. The needles were left in place for 30 minutes and were stimulated once every 10 minutes. One treatment was given per day and 10 treatments equalled one course of therapy. After one course, the patient was allowed to rest for 3–5 days before starting a new course of therapy.

Supplementally, in order to strengthen the treatment effect and depending on the patient's pattern and signs and symptoms, small seeds or pellets were taped to one or more of the following ear acupuncture points: *Shen Men* (Spirit Gate), Subcortex, Heart, Liver, Spleen, or Kidneys. Up to six of these ear points were selected. The patient was instructed to press each of these pellets four times each day in order to stimulate these points. The points were pressed before sleep, after waking, in the morning, and in the afternoon. Both ears were treated at the same time.

Cure was defined as being able to go to sleep easily and staying asleep for seven hours or more. Marked effect meant that one could go to sleep relatively easily and could stay asleep for more than five hours. Some effect meant that the symptoms were decreased but the condition relapsed. No effect meant that the condition was the same as before treatment. Based on these criteria, after two whole courses of therapy, 14 cases or 63.64% were cured; five cases or 22.73% noticed a marked effect; and three cases or 13.63% saw some effect. Therefore, the total effectiveness rate was 100%. Further, more than half these cases took an obvious turn for the better after a single treatment.

'Joining Needling at *Nei Guan* (Per 6) in the Treatment of 202 Cases of Insomnia' by Liu Bing-quan, *Xin Zhong Yi* (*New Chinese Medicine*), No. 5, 1996, p. 34

Of the 202 patients studied in this clinical audit, 82 were male and 120 were female. Their ages ranged from 18 to 65, with the majority being between 30 and 45 years old. In 54 cases, their course of disease has lasted six months to one year. In 128 cases, it had lasted one to three years. And in 20 cases, it had lasted for more than three years. Eighty-five per cent of these patients continued to take or intermittently took sleeping medications. These 202 patients were divided into two groups of 101 patients each for comparison purposes.

In terms of their diagnostic criteria, these patients all suffered from inability to go to sleep, difficulty going to sleep, sometimes sleeping and sometimes being aroused, difficulty sleeping after being aroused, or sleep diminished by 40%. In some cases, they could only go to sleep after taking sleeping medication. Most of these patients also had varying degrees of dizziness, headache, heart palpitations and impaired memory.

In one group, called the Needling *Nei Guan* Group, the treatment method consisted of acupuncturing *Nei Guan* (Per 6) to a depth of 20–25mm/0.8–1in deep along with the points *Shen Men* (Ht 7) and *Tai Chong* (Liv 3). In the second group, called the Joining Needling *Nei Guan* Group, *Nei Guan* was needled deeply through to *Wai Guan* (TB 5) but without breaking the skin on the opposite side of the forearm. After obtaining the needling sensation the needles were stimulated once every 10 minutes with even supplementing/even draining technique. The needles were retained for 30 minutes per treatment with one treatment given per day. Thirty such treatments equalled one course of therapy.

Patients were considered cured if their sleep increased to 70–80% per night or more and they could stop taking sleeping medication. Marked effect meant that sleep increased to 60–70% and they could stop taking sleeping medication. Some effect meant that sleep increased to 50–60% per night and they could stop taking sleeping medication. No effect meant that sleep per night was only 40% or below and patients had to continue taking their sleeping medication.

Based on these criteria, in the Joining Needling Group, 35 cases were cured, 34 saw a marked effect, 20 saw some effect, and 12 had no effect. Thus the total improvement rate for this group was 88.1%. In the *Nei Guan* Group, 20 were cured, 16 saw marked effect, 40 saw some effect, and 25 had no effect. Therefore, the total improvement rate in this group was 75.2%. Thus both these treatments were considered statistically significantly effective.

'A Survey of the Treatment Efficacy of Treating Recalcitrant Insomnia with *Xue Fu Zhu Yu Tang* (Blood Mansion Dispel Stasis Decoction)' by Zhan Guo-tong, *Xin Zhong Yi* (*New Chinese Medicine*), 1996, No. 8, pp. 32–33

Of the 31 patients in this clinical audit, 26 were outpatients and five were inpatients. There were 11 males and 20 females. Three were between 15 and 30 years of age; eight were between 31 and 40; eight were between 41 and 50; nine were between 51 and 60, and three were 61 years old or older. Their course of disease had lasted six months to one year in five cases, from one to five years in 17 cases, from five to ten years in seven cases, and for more than 10 years in two cases.

All the patients in this study exhibited varying degrees of blood stasis, such as piercing pain in the head, dizziness, static macules on their tongues and a choppy pulse. In addition, four other patterns were also discriminated: qi vacuity and blood stasis (11 cases), blood vacuity and blood stasis (8 cases), yin vacuity and blood stasis (6 cases), and phlegm heat and blood stasis (6 cases).

Based on everyone in this study suffering from blood stasis as at least part of the mechanisms of their insomnia, *Xue Fu Zhu Yu Tang* (Blood Mansion Dispel Stasis Decoction) was used as the guiding prescription. This was then modified for each of the four complicating patterns. The basic formula consisted of:

Semen Pruni Persicae (*Tao Ren*), Flos Carthami Tinctorii (*Hong Hua*), Radix Angelicae Sinensis (*Dang Gui*), Fructus Citri Aurantii (*Zhi Ke*), Radix Rubrus Paeoniae Lactiflorae (*Chi Shao*), Radix Platycodi Grandiflori (*Jie Geng*), 10g/2tsp each, uncooked Radix Rehmanniae (*Sheng Di*), 15g/1tbsp, Radix Achyranthis Bidentatae (*Niu Xi*), 6g/1tsp, Caulis Polygoni Multiflori (*Ye Jiao Teng*), 30g/2tbsp, Succinum (*Hu Po*), 1.5g/¼tsp, uncooked Radix Glycyrrhizae (*Gan Cao*), 3g/½tsp.

If there was concomitant qi vacuity, Radix Codonopsitis Pilosulae (*Dang Shen*), 10g/2tsp, and mix-fried Radix Astragali Membranacei (*Huang Qi*), 50g/2oz, were added. If there was concomitant blood vacuity, cooked Radix Rehmanniae (*Shu Di*), 25g/1oz, and Gelatinum Corii Asini (*E Jiao*), 10g/2tsp, were added. If there was simultaneous yin vacuity, Fructus Lycii Chinensis (*Gou Qi Zi*), 15g/1tbsp, Fructus Corni Officinalis (*Shan Zhu Yu*), 12g/2½tsp, Rhizoma Acori Graminei (*Shi Chang Pu*), 6g/1tsp, Radix Polygalae Tenuifoliae (*Yuan Zhi*), 5g/1tsp, Radix Glehniae Littoralis (*Bei Sha Shen*), and Tuber Ophiopogonis Japonici (*Mai Dong*), 10g/2tsp each, were added. If there was simultaneous phlegm heat, Pericarpium Citri Reticulatae (*Chen Pi*), 10g/2tsp, Rhizoma Pinelliae Ternatae (*Ban Xia*) and processed Rhizoma Arisaematis (*Nan Xing*), 12g/2½tsp each, and Radix Scutellariae Baicalensis (*Huang Qin*) and Tuber Curcumae (*Yu Jin*), 10g/2tsp each, were added. These were decocted in water and administered, one packet per day in two divided doses, morning and evening.

Cure meant that the patients were able to fall asleep easily each evening and sleep for eight hours or more. In addition, all their other symptoms disappeared. Marked effect meant that patients could sleep for at least six hours each evening and the major part of their accompanying symptoms disappeared. Some effect meant that the patients' sleep each night was longer than before. However, it still remained less than six hours. Or it meant that some of their symptoms disappeared. No effect meant that there was no change for the better in sleep and no improvement in symptoms.

Based on the above criteria, of the patients in the qi vacuity pattern group, six were cured, three saw marked improvement, and two noticed some effect. In the yin vacuity group, three were cured, two registered marked improvement, and one saw some effect. Of the patients in the blood vacuity group, six were cured and two registered marked improvement. And of those in the phlegm heat group, one was cured, three saw some effect, and two saw no effect. Therefore, using this protocol, those patients in the blood vacuity/blood stasis group got the best results and those in the phlegm heat/blood stasis group got the worst. Twenty-four cases were followed up from one to three years, and only two cases had relapsed. The cure rate was 51.6% and the total effectiveness rate was 93.5%.

'The Treatment of 12 Cases of Recalcitrant Insomnia by Tapping the Governing Vessel' by Zhuang Dan-hong, *Hei Long Jiang Zhong Yi Yao* (*Heilongjiang Chinese Medicine and Medicinals*), 1996, No. 3, p. 47

Eight of the patients in this study were male and four were female. All were young, seemingly healthy adults. Ten cases suffered from overtaxation due to too much study and 'brain work'. Two cases were workers. The treatment method consisted of first disinfecting the skin over the vertebrae from the neck to the sacrum. Then a small hammer with several small needles embedded in its head was used to tap up and down over the governing vessel on the midline of the back. This tapping was continued until either the area tapped was flushed red or there was very, very slight bleeding. This was done once each day. All the patients in this study were cured using this technique.

By way of example, the author gives a case history. The patient was a 34-year-old male who worked as a teacher. He had suffered from recurrent insomnia for four years which was lately even more severe. He had difficulty falling asleep, dizziness, heart palpitations, lack of strength of his entire body, poor appetite, constipation, reddish coloured urine, a red tongue with yellow fur and a fine, rapid pulse. He had previously been administered a couple of different Chinese herbal decoctions which had not proved particularly effective. This had been combined with oral administration of Western sleep medication which had put him to sleep. When he decided to come to the hospital for acupuncture treatment he had stopped taking these sleep medications and he was only sleeping approximately three hours per night. After being treated with the above protocol 2–3 times, his sleep increased to 4–5 hours. He stopped taking the Chinese medicinals and his treatment was stabilised after three more treatments, at which time he was discharged from the hospital.

The author says that insomnia is mostly due to yin vacuity with yang hyperactivity. Tapping the governing vessel like this regulates yin and yang, rectifies the qi and blood, harmonises the viscera and bowels, and frees the flow of the channels and network vessels. When the tapping causes a little bleeding, it further drains yang heat which is hyperactive and exuberant. This then has the effect of levelling or calming yin and secreting yang. As it is said, 'When yin is levelled and yang secreted, the essence spirit (i.e., the mind) is treated (i.e., cured).'

MORE CASE HISTORIES

In order to help readers get a better feel for how Chinese medicine treats insomnia, I have given below some more case histories. These are true stories of people who have benefited from treatment with acupuncture and/or Chinese herbal medicine for insomnia. It is my hope that you will be able to recognise some of your symptoms in these cases and be encouraged to try acupuncture and Chinese herbal medicine.

GARY

Gary was a 34-year-old publisher whose main problem was insomnia. Three months before coming for treatment, he had been assigned to oversee a very important job with a very tight deadline. He had worked around the clock for a whole week. Due to this intense mental and physical strain, he found it progressively harder and harder to fall asleep. Most nights he would toss and turn for three or four hours before finally sinking into the 'sweet balm' of sleep. However, once asleep, he had disturbing dreams and was easily awakened. On really bad nights, Gary was only able to sleep for two or three hours. Then, the next day, he felt tired and dizzy and particularly weak in his low back region and knees.

When Gary was questioned, his Chinese Medicine Practitioner found that he had been suffering from frequent night sweats along with the insomnia and that he was now plagued with premature ejaculation when he had sex with his girlfriend. He had tried some Western tranquillisers. If he took the prescribed dose, they didn't work, but if he took a double dose, he was groggy and couldn't think straight all the next day. Recently, he had rearranged his work schedule and tried to relax. However, so far, his insomnia had not improved. On examination, Gary's tongue had a red tip with a thin tongue coating and his pulse had a thready quality.

Gary's Chinese pattern discrimination was loss of interaction between the heart and kidneys. The treatment principles were to restore the interaction between the heart and kidneys by nourishing kidney yin, clearing heat fire, and leading yang back to its lower source. Gary was given the following Chinese medicinal prescription:

cooked Radix Rehmanniae (*Shu Di*), 12g/2½tsp
Radix Dioscoreae Oppositae (*Shan Yao*), 9g/1¾tsp
Fructus Corni Officinalis (*Shan Zhu Yu*), 9g/1¾tsp
Sclerotium Poriae Cocos (*Fu Ling*), 9g/1¾tsp
Fructus Schisandrae Chinensis (*Wu Wei Zi*), 9g/1¾tsp
Cortex Radicis Moutan (*Dan Pi*), 9g/1¾tsp
Rhizoma Alismatis (*Ze Xie*), 9g/1¾tsp
Cortex Cinnamomi Cassiae (*Rou Gui*), 6g/1tsp
Rhizoma Coptidis Chinensis (*Huang Lian*), 3g/½ tsp

The above Chinese medicinals were decocted in water and administered in two divided doses per day after lunch and dinner. In addition, Gary was instructed on how to tape magnets over *Shen Mai* (Bl 62) and *Zhao Hai* (Ki 6) before bed each night. He was told to stay away from hot, spicy food, fried, fatty foods, alcohol and all stimulants such as coffee, tea or chocolate.

After taking the above Chinese medicinals, Gary returned to the clinic to report that he was now sleeping five or more hours each night and that he fell asleep easily within half an hour of going to bed. After two weeks' administration of the above formula, he was able to sleep normally throughout the night, getting a full seven hours' sleep. His tongue no longer had a red tip and his other symptoms had all markedly improved.

PRISCILLA

Priscilla was 52 years old. She had been suffering from insomnia for two years. This had begun shortly after she had ceased menstruation. Like Gary, Priscilla also had night sweats along with her insomnia. Although Priscilla had some trouble going to sleep, her real difficulty was staying asleep. She would typically sleep for four hours and then wake without being able to go back to sleep. Thus, she would toss and turn restlessly until daybreak when she would get up and go about her day.

Besides matitudinal insomnia and night sweats, Priscilla had hot flushes during the day. She would not only feel flushed in the face, but the palms of her hands and soles of her feet would feel hot. At night, however, her feet would be as cold as ice. When she woke up in the early morning hours, it was typically to urinate. All her life she had been able to sleep through the night without having to go to the bathroom, but now she would urinate at least once and often twice each night. In addition, Priscilla complained of a chronically sore low back and no interest in sex whatsoever. This latter was also a change from before menopause. On inspection, Priscilla's tongue also had a red tip, but its body was paler than normal and its fur was scanty and dry. Priscilla's pulse quality was thready bowstring and rapid overall. In particular, her pulse positions corresponding to the kidneys were floating as well.

Taken as a whole, these signs and symptoms added up to liver–blood–kidney yin and yang vacuity with vacuity heat disturbing the heart spirit above. The treatment principles were to enrich the kidneys and nourish the liver, invigorate yang and clear vacuity heat above. The formula she was given contained the following ingredients:

Rhizoma Curculiginis Orchioidis (_Xian Mao_), 9g/1¾tsp
Herba Epimedii (_Xian Ling Pi_), 9g/1¾tsp
Radix Angelicae Sinensis (_Dang Gui_), 9g/1¾tsp

Rhizoma Anemarrhenae Aspheloidis (*Zhi Mu*), 9g/1¾tsp
Cortex Phellodendri (*Huang Bai*), 9g/1¾tsp
Fructus Levis Tritici Aestivi (*Fu Xiao Mai*), 45g/3tbsp
Fructus Schisandrae Chinensis (*Wu Wei Zi*), 9g/1¾tsp
Concha Ostreae (*Mu Li*), 18g/3½tsp
Herba Ecliptae Prostratae (*Han Lian Cao*), 15g/1tbsp
Fructus Ligustri Lucidi (*Nu Zhen Zi*), 15g/1tbsp

Priscilla took this prescription the same way that Gary did above. She also received press needles in the ear acupuncture points *Shen Men* (Spirit Gate), Internal Secretion, Adrenals and Kidneys, two points in one ear and the other two in the other ear. Priscilla was instructed to press each of these needles four times each day: before bed, after rising, in the morning, and in the afternoon. She was asked to drink a warm glass of boiled milk containing a whole whipped egg.

Within a week, Priscilla reported that her feet were no longer cold and that she was no longer getting up to urinate at night. Since she was not being awoken to urinate, she was sleeping six or seven hours each night instead of four. In order to consolidate this treatment, Priscilla received weekly body acupuncture for another six weeks, and she was given the core prescription above as a patent pill. This resulted in her hot flushes and night sweats going away. Her interest in sex returned, much to the delight of herself and her husband.

CAROLYN

Carolyn was 32 years old. A year ago she had decided to do further training. She had been studying hard with considerable mental strain. She was a single mother, a breadwinner, and a student at the same time, which was not easy. Carolyn began to suffer from insomnia. She had great difficulty falling asleep and tossed and turned for hours each night. When she was able to fall asleep, she had nightmares and other very vivid, very disturbing dreams. Often she would wake in a startle, her heart pounding. In college, she noticed that her memory was getting worse, instead of better.

When questioned by her Chinese Medicine Practitioner, Carolyn reported that she suffered from heart palpitations, restlessness, shortness of breath and was feeling very withdrawn and uncommunicative. When she was pressed by others into talking, she often became irritable. She was generally fatigued and occasionally had night sweats, especially during her menstruation. Sometimes she had a good appetite, but other times she didn't have the energy to eat. Her bowel movements and urination were both normal and her menstrual cycle was regular. Since having her little girl two years previously, Carolyn had noticed that the volume of her menses was definitely reduced. For the last year, she had noticed that her insomnia was worse before and during her period and that she had pre-menstrual breast distension and discomfort which disappeared as soon as her menses came. On inspection, Carolyn's tongue was red at the tip and had yellow, slimy fur. Her pulse was bowstring, thready and rapid.

Carolyn's Chinese pattern discrimination was depressive heat disturbing her heart spirit complicated by qi and blood vacuity. The treatment principles were to course the liver and rectify the qi, clear heat and resolve depression, supplement the qi and blood and quiet the spirit. Carolyn was given body acupuncture every other day, three days a week at the following points:

Tai Chong (Liv 3)
San Yin Jiao (Sp 6)
Zu San Li (St 36)
Shen Men (Ht 7)
Nei Guan (Per 6)
Shan Zhong (CV 17)
Feng Chi (GB 20)
Si Shen Cong (M-HN-1)

She was also prescribed the following Chinese medicinals to be taken as a water-boiled decoction:

Radix Bupleuri (*Chai Hu*), 9g/1¾tsp
Cortex Radicis Moutan (*Dan Pi*), 9g/1¾tsp
Fructus Gardeniae Jasminoidis (*Shan Zhi Zi*), 9g/1¾tsp
Rhizoma Coptidis Chinensis (*Huang Lian*), 4.5g/¾tsp
Cortex Albizziae Julibrissin (*He Huan Pi*), 9g/1¾tsp
Caulis Polygoni Multiflori (*Ye Jiao Teng*), 9g/1¾tsp
Rhizoma Atractylodis Macrocephalae (*Bai Zhu*), 9g/1¾tsp
Sclerotium Poriae Cocos (*Fu Ling*), 12g/2tsp
Fructus Tritici Aestivi (*Huai Xiao Mai*), 30g/2tbsp
mix-fried Radix Glycyrrhizae (*Gan Cao*), 9g/1¾tsp
Fructus Zizyphi Jujubae (*Da Zao*), 10 pieces
Radix Angelicae Sinensis (*Dang Gui*), 9g/1¾tsp
Radix Albus Paeoniae Lactiflorae (*Bai Shao*), 18g/3½tsp

Further, Carolyn was given some Lignum Aquilariae Agallochae (*Chen Xiang*) to burn as incense while she was going to bed at night. After three treatments and four days of taking the above Chinese medicinal formula, Carolyn was able to sleep through the night. In order to consolidate the treatment effect, she was given *Dan Zhi Xiao Yao Wan* (Moutan and Gardenia Rambling Pills) to continue coursing the liver and clearing heat at the same time as supplementing the qi and blood. She was also advised to come in for two or three acupuncture treatments in the week before her menstruation for two or three cycles, since this was the time her insomnia tended to be at its worst. Carolyn was advised on a regular exercise programme and provided with a deep relaxation tape for daily practice. After three menstrual cycles, Carolyn had no more insomnia, her mood was improved, and she had no further pre-menstrual breast distenstion or pain. Her concentration at college improved. Six months later, she reconciled with her little girl's father.

MIKE

Mike was 54 years old and had been suffering from insomnia for a year. He usually woke between 3 and 4 a.m. and then found it difficult to fall back asleep. During the day, Mike felt drowsy, he felt dizzy if he stood up quickly and he had a poor memory. Ever since developing insomnia, his appetite had been poor, and, if he ate a good-sized meal, his abdomen would become bloated and he would feel full and uncomfortable. Although Mike felt fatigued, he did not feel restless or agitated. His tongue was enlarged with toothmarks along its edges. The fur was thin and white, but the tongue's colour was very noticeably pale. Mike's pulse was quite thready and not very forceful for a man. Mike had been a strict vegan, eating no animal products for the previous 11 years.

Mike's signs and symptoms add up to heart–blood–spleen qi vacuity. The treatment principles were to nourish the heart, fortify the spleen and quiet the spirit. This pattern is usually a very easy type of insomnia to treat. It typically responds well to Chinese herbal medicine. Hence Mike was prescribed:

Radix Astragali Membranacei _(Huang Qi)_, 18g/3½tsp
Radix Panacis Ginseng _(Ren Shen)_, 6g/1tsp
Rhizoma Atractylodis Macrocephalae _(Bai Zhu)_, 9g/1¾tsp
Sclerotium Pararadicis Poriae Cocos _(Fu Shen)_, 12g/2tsp
mix-fried Radix Glycyrrhizae _(Gan Cao)_, 9g/1¾tsp
Fructus Zizyphi Jujubae _(Da Zao)_, 6 pieces
Semen Zizyphi Spinosae _(Suan Zao Ren)_, 15g/1tbsp
Semen Biotae Orientalis _(Bai Zi Ren)_, 12g/2tsp
Radix Angelicae Sinensis _(Dang Gui)_, 9g/1¾tsp
Radix Polygalae Tenuifoliae _(Yuan Zhi)_, 9g/1¾tsp
Radix Auklandiae Lappae _(Mu Xiang)_, 9g/1¾tsp

Mike took this formula as a water-boiled decoction for two weeks. He was also convinced to add some beef broth and marrow bone soup to his regular diet as well as an occasional egg. He was instructed how to prepare Semen Zizyphi Spinosae (*Suan Zao Ren*) and rice, Semen Biotae Orientalis (*Bai Zi Ren*) and rice, and Sclerotium Poriae Cocos (*Fu Ling*) and rice porridge. After two weeks, he was sleeping through the night. His tongue was not so pale and he reported that he had more energy than he had had for years. In order to keep Mike moving in the right direction, he was instructed to take *Gui Pi Wan* (Restore the Spleen Pills) for 25 out of every 30 days each month for the next few months. On follow-up one year later, there had been no recurrence. Interestingly, on follow-up, Mike reported that his night vision had markedly improved and now he did not hesitate to drive at night.

ANNA

Anna was 87 years old. She had had insomnia for years and years. When she lay down at night to sleep, she couldn't stand having anything lying on her chest, and she could never go to sleep if she did not take some sleeping medication. Anna commonly experienced chest pain, chest oppression and vexatious heat within her heart. At dawn she would often find herself covered in sweat. Her mind was always busy and her heart frequently skipped beats. Besides a bound, slow and irregular pulse, Anna's pulse was also bowstring, while her tongue was purplish red.

Anna's pattern is a common one in older patients suffering from insomnia. Due to her age and the declining function of the heart and lungs, the blood tends to become static. This static blood then impedes the creation of fresh or new blood. This leads to blood and yin vacuity with vacuity heat in the heart disturbing the spirit. The treatment principles in Anna's case were to nourish and quicken the blood, course and disinhibit the hundreds of vessels, clear the heart and quiet the spirit. The prescription written for Anna consisted of:

uncooked Radix Rehmanniae (*Sheng Di*), 9g/1¾tsp
Radix Angelicae Sinensis (*Dang Gui*), 9g/1¾tsp
Radix Rubrus Paeoniae Lactiflorae (*Chi Shao*), 9g/1¾tsp
Radix Ligustici Wallichii (*Chuan Xiong*), 6g/1tsp
Flos Carthami Tinctorii (*Hong Hua*), 9g/1¾tsp
Semen Pruni Persicae (*Tao Ren*), 9g/1¾tsp
Radix Bupleuri (*Chai Hu*), 4.5g/¾tsp
Radix Platycodi Grandiflori (*Jie Geng*), 4.5g/¾tsp
Fructus Citri Aurantii (*Zhi Ke*), 4.5g/¾tsp
Radix Achyranthis Bidentatae (*Niu Xi*), 6g/1tsp
Rhizoma Coptidis Chinensis (*Huang Lian*), 1.5g/¼tsp
Succinum (*Hu Po*), 4.5g/¾tsp
Radix Glycyrrhizae (*Gan Cao*), 3g/½tsp

All the above ingredients except the Succinum (powdered Amber) were decocted in water and taken in three divided doses beginning at lunch. This meant that the last dose was given about half an hour before bed. At this time, Anna used the decocted medicinals to wash down the powdered Succinum. Since neither blood vacuity nor blood stasis respond all that quickly to acupuncture, Anna was not needled. Rather, she was encouraged to A) get a massage once a week and B) take this formula for at least one month before passing judgement. Anna said that she hadn't been able to sleep on her own for years in any case, so she didn't mind waiting a little longer before she could go to sleep on her own.

After one month of taking the above medicinals, Anna was able to go to sleep without Western sedatives three out of every five nights. Anna was also very happy that she was not having so many chest pains or palpitations. Her doctor was quite impressed by the changes in Anna's heart beat when he listened to it at her next checkup. When Anna told him about the Chinese medicinals she had been taking, he said these changes may have only been a 'coincidence'. As Anna left the surgery, he said, 'If I were you, I'd keep taking those Chinese herbs whatever they are.'

As the above case histories show, Chinese medicine treats the whole person. This is not just symptomatic treatment. In all the above cases, the patients not only achieved better sleep but some or all of their other symptoms and problems also improved.

Although Chinese medicine does not work as immediately as Western sedatives, the benefits are much more real and long-lasting, and they are also without side effects. Once someone understands that this is not a quick fix they are often motivated to make changes to their diet and lifestyle, especially when they start to experience the benefits of treatment.

FINDING A PRACTITIONER

Chinese medicine has grown enormously in the UK during the past 30 years. There are at least ten colleges which offer professional training, some offering a university degree.

Many excellent practitioners have come to the UK from China, Vietnam and other countries of East Asia.

As you will have no doubt realised after reading this book, Chinese medicine is a whole system of medicine with its own fundamental concepts and theories. It is not simply a technique. Previous knowledge or training in another system of medicine does not automatically confer competence or knowledge in Chinese medicine. In order to get the most out of your therapy or treatment you should make sure that the practitioner is properly qualified. Currently in the UK the onus is on individuals to check the qualifications and training of their practitioner. In order to help you to do this we have listed the relevant professional bodies covering Chinese medicine. Members of these professional organisations are bound by a professional code of ethics and practice. They will have received an accredited level of training and will be covered by medical malpractice and public/products liability insurance.

When trying to find a good practitioner, one of the best methods is word of mouth. It is also important that you are able to communicate with the practitioner, should English not be their first language. It is fine to ask about their previous experience in treating your complaint. Many practitioners will be happy to talk on the phone or may offer a short introductory consultation so that you can assess whether you will feel comfortable working with them.

We have included Japanese traditions of herbal medicine (kanpo) and massage (shiatsu) in addition to Chinese. They originate from the same basic sources but have evolved differently in terms of style of practice.

The relevant professional bodies for Chinese medicine in the UK are:

Acupuncture
The British Acupuncture Council
63 Jeddo Road, London W12 9HQ
Tel: 020 8735 0400
Fax: 020 7735 0404
e-mail: info@acupuncture.org.uk
website: www.acupuncture.org.uk
Members have the initials MBAcC.

Chinese herbal medicine
The Register of Chinese Herbal Medicine
PO Box 400, Wembley, Middlesex HA9 9NZ
Tel/Fax: 07000 790332
website: www.rchm.co.uk
Members have the initials MRCHM.

Japanese herbal medicine – Kanpo
The Kanpo Association
9a Ingatestone Road, Brentwood, Essex CM15 8AP
Tel: 01277 260080
Members have the initials KANPO.

Most members of the Kanpo Association are also members of the RCHM. They are not bound by a code of ethics and practice unless they are members of another professional body.

Shiatsu
The Shiatsu Society UK
Barber House, Storeys Bar Road
Fengate, Peterborough PE1 5YS
Tel: 01733 758341
e-mail: shiatsu@graphic-scan.co.uk
Members have the initials MRSS.

AUSTRALIA
Acupuncture Association of Victoria
126 Union Road, Surrey Hills
Victoria 3127
Tel: 1800 025 334

Australia Acupuncture Ethics and Standards Organisation
PO Box 84, Merrylands
New South Wales 2160
Tel: 1800 025 334

Australia Traditional Medicine Society
120 Blaxland Road, Ryde
New South Wales 2112
Tel: 1800 809 6800

SOUTH AFRICA
Chiropractic, Homeopathic and
Allied Health Services Professional Services
PO Box 17005, Groenkloof 0027

The International Institute of Chinese Medicine
and Acupuncture
PO Box 2246, 19 Av Disandt-Fresnaye,
Cape Town 8000
Tel: 27 21 434 1654

LEARNING MORE ABOUT
CHINESE MEDICINE

For more information about Chinese medicine in general, see:
Chinese Medicine: Acupuncture, Herbal Remedies, Nutrition, Qi Gong and Meditation by Tom Williams, Element Health Essentials. This is a good basic introduction to the whole field of Chinese medicine for the layperson.

Acupuncture by Peter Mole, Element Books. A simple and clear introduction to acupuncture for the layperson.

A Guide to Acupuncture by Peter Firebrace and Sandra Hill, Constable Books. A comprehensive introduction to acupuncture for the layperson with some illustrations and photographs.

Between Heaven and Earth: A Guide to Chinese Medicine by Harriet Beinfield and Efrem Korngold, Ballantine Books, New York. This book is particularly good with regard to the more psychological and emotional aspects of Chinese medicine and has a good introduction to herbal medicine for the layperson.

Acupuncture in Practice edited by Hugh McPherson and Ted Kaptchuk, Churchill Livingston. This is a book of case histories from the West; it illustrates the wide variety of styles and methods of practice of acupuncture by many well-known practitioners.

Chinese Herbal Medicine, a practical guide to the healing powers of herbs by Dr Guang Xu, Vermillion. A good introduction to Chinese herbal medicine.

Japanese Acupuncture a Clinical Guide, by Stephen Birch and Junko Ida, Paradigm Publications. This book gives very good clear details on moxibustion.

For more information on dietary therapy, see:
Healing with Wholefoods, Oriental Traditions and Modern Nutrition by Paul Pritchard, North Atlantic Books. A comprehensive source book for both the layperson and the professional.

Helping Ourselves: A Guide to Traditional Chinese Food Energetics by Daverick Legget, Meridian Press. This book is designed for ease of use with its clear layout and wall charts.

For more information on qi gong, see:
Stand Still be Fit: The Way of Energy by Master Lam Kam Chuen, Gaia. This is a very popular book and accompanying videotape which demonstrates qi gong exercises.

SUPPLIERS OF CHINESE HERBS

In the UK it is not possible to buy Chinese herbal medicines as a member of the public. You will need a prescription from a qualified Chinese herbalist. Some acupuncturists are able to prescribe traditional remedies or 'patents'. The suppliers we have listed here are members of CMAS – The Chinese Medicine Association of Suppliers. CMAS is a professional organisation which acts as a self-regulatory body to lobby in the interest of its members within the bounds of public safety. All members are subject to a code of practice. CMAS is a new organisation and rapidly growing so it may have more members since this list was completed.

Many of the members of CMAS have an excellent supply of books and other products relating to Chinese medicine/ acupuncture. Most if not all suppliers have a mail order service.

This list is by no means exhaustive. There are many other suppliers of acupuncture products and many shops which sell Chinese herbs. The acupuncture product suppliers are a good source should you wish to buy the seven star hammer mentioned in the chapter on home remedies. The Chinese herbal medicine shops one sees on many high streets may not be regulated.

Acumedic (MF Mei, Director)
101–105 Camden High Street
London NW1 7JN
Tel: 020 7388 5783
Fax: 020 7387 5766

Beijing Tong Ren Tang
(Laurence Lo, Director)
124 Shaftesbury Avenue
London W1V 7DJ
Tel: 020 7287 0098
Fax: 020 7287 0068

China Medica
25 Lonsdale Close
London SE9 4HF
Tel: 020 8857 9777
Fax: 020 8480 2020

Chinese Medical Centre
179 South Street, Romford
Essex RM1 1PS
Tel: 01708 756363
Fax: 01708 703015

East West Herbs
Langston Priory Mews, Kingham
Oxfordshire OX7 6UP
Tel: 01608 658862
Fax: 01608 658816
e-mail:
robert@eastwestherbs.co.uk

Great Wall
Unit 27, Riverside Works,
Hertford Road
Barking IG11 8BN
Tel: 020 8591 6896
Fax: 020 8591 6891

Harmony Medical Distribution
629 High Road, Leytonstone
London E11 4PA
Tel: 020 8518 7337
Fax: 020 8556 5038
e-mail: harmony@tcm.org.uk

Healthpack Ltd
Langston Priory Mews, Kingham
Oxfordshire OX7 6UP
Tel: 01608 658862
Fax: 01608 658816

Lotus
Priorsfield Priory
Forest Row, Sussex RH18 5HR
Tel: 01342 823053

Mayway UK
43 Waterside Trading Centre
Trumpers Way, Hanwell
Middlesex
Tel: 020 8893 6873

Number One Herb Co
36 Bankhurst Road
London SE6 4XN
Tel: 020 8690 4840

Oxford Medical Supplies
Units 11 & 12 Horcott Industrial
Estate
Fairford, Gloucestershire
Tel: 0800 975 8000

Shizhen TCM UK Ltd
50 Sandy Lane, Chorlton
Manchester M21
Tel: 0161 881 0088

Tian Tiao Ltd
83 Sullivan Way, Elstree
Herts WD6 3DG

Naturally Chinese
PO Box 4584, Kiln Farm
Milton Keynes
Bucks MK13 9ZT
Tel: 0151 571 0407

CHINESE MEDICAL GLOSSARY

Chinese medicine is a system unto itself. Its technical terms are uniquely its own and cannot be translated into the definitions of Western medicine without destroying their very fabric and logic. Ultimately, because Chinese medicine was created in the Chinese language, it is best understood in that language. Nevertheless, as Westerners trying to understand Chinese medicine, we must translate the technical terms of Chinese medicine in English words. If some of these technical translations sound at first peculiar and their meaning is not immediately transparent, this is because no equivalent concepts exist in every-day English.

In the past, some Western authors have erroneously translated technical Chinese medical terms using Western medical or at least quasi-scientific words in an attempt to make this system more easily understood by Western audiences. For instance, the words tonify and sedate are commonly seen in the Western Chinese medical literature even though, in the case of sedate, its meaning is the opposite to the Chinese understanding of the word *xie*. *Xie* means to drain off something which has pooled and accumulated. That accumulation is seen as something excess which should not be lingering where it is. Because it is accumulating somewhere where it shouldn't, it is impeding and obstructing whatever should be moving to and through that area. The word sedate comes from the Latin word *sedere*, to sit. Therefore, the word sedate means to make something sit still. In English, we get the word sediment from this same root. However, the Chinese *xie* means draining off something which is sitting somewhere erroneously. This mistranslation could be potentially misleading in terms of its clinical applications.

Therefore, in order, to preserve the integrity of this system while still making it intelligible to English language readers, I have appended the following glossary of Chinese medical technical terms. The terms themselves are based on Nigel Wiseman's *English–Chinese Chinese–English Dictionary of Chinese Medicine* published by the Hunan Science and Technology Press in Changsha, Hunan, People's Republic of China in 1995. Dr Wiseman is, in my opinion, the greatest Western scholar in terms of the translation of Chinese medicine into English. As a Chinese reader myself, although I often find Wiseman's terms awkward-sounding at first, I also think they convey most accurately the Chinese understanding and logic of these terms.

Acquired essence: Essence manufactured out of the surplus of qi and blood in turn created out of the refined essence of food and drink.

Acupoints: Those places on the channels and network vessels where qi and blood tend to collect in denser concentrations, and thus those places where the qi and blood in the channels are especially available for manipulation.

Acupuncture: The regulation of qi flow by the stimulation of certain points located on the channels and network vessels achieved mainly by the insertion of fine needles into these points.

Aromatherapy: Using various scents and smells to treat and prevent illness.

Ascendant hyperactivity of liver yang: Upwardly out of control counterflow of liver yang due to insufficient yin to hold it down in the lower part of the body.

Blood: The red-coloured fluid which flows in the vessels and nourishes and constructs the tissues of the body.

Blood stasis: Also called dead blood, malign blood and dry blood, blood stasis is blood which is no longer moving through the vessels as it should. Instead it is precipitated in the vessels like silt in a river. Like silt, it then obstructs the free flow of the blood in the vessels and also impedes the production of new or fresh blood.

Blood vacuity: Insufficient blood manifesting in diminished nourishment, construction and moistening of body tissues.

Bowels: The hollow yang organs of Chinese medicine.

Channels: The main routes for the distribution of qi and blood, but mainly qi.

Clear: The pure or clear part of food and drink ingested which is then turned into qi and blood.

Counterflow: An erroneous flow of qi, usually upwards but sometimes horizontally as well.

Dampness: A pathological accumulation of body fluids.

Decoction: A method of administering Chinese medicinals by boiling these medicinals in water, removing the dregs and drinking the resulting medicinal liquid.

Depression: Stagnation and lack of movement, as in liver depression qi stagnation.

Drain: To drain off or away some pathological qi or substance from where it is replete or excessive.

Essence: A stored, very potent form of substance and qi, usually yin when compared to yang qi, but can be transformed into yang qi.

Five phase theory: An ancient Chinese system of correspondences dividing up all of reality into five phases which then mutually engender and check each other according to definite sequences.

Hydrotherapy: Using various baths and water applications to treat and prevent disease.

Life gate fire: Another name for kidney yang or kidney fire, seen as the ultimate source of yang qi in the body.

Magnet therapy: Applying magnets to acupuncture points to treat and prevent disease.

Moxibustion: Burning the herb Artemisia Argyium on, over or near acupuncture points in order to add yang qi, warm cold or promote the movement of the qi and blood.

Network vessels: Small vessels which form a net-like web ensuring the flow of qi and blood to all body tissues.

Phlegm: A pathological accumulation of phlegm or mucus congealed from dampness or body fluids.

Portals: Also called orifices, the openings of the sensory organs and the opening of the heart through which the spirit makes contact with the world outside.

Qi: Activity, function, that which moves, transforms, defends, restrains and warms.

Qi mechanism: The process of transforming yin substance controlled and promoted by the qi, largely synonymous with the process of digestion.

Qi vacuity: Insufficient qi manifesting in diminished movement, transformation and function.

Repletion: Excess or fullness, almost always pathological.

Seven star hammer: A small hammer with needles embedded in its head used to stimulate acupoints without actually inserting needles.

Spirit: The accumulation of qi in the heart which manifests as consciousness, sensory awareness and mental-emotional function.

Stagnation: Non-movement of the qi, lack of free flow, constraint.

Supplement: To add to or augment, as in supplementing the qi, blood, yin or yang.

Turbid: The yin, impure, turbid part of food and drink which is sent downwards to be excreted as waste.

Vacuity: Emptiness or insufficiency, typically of qi, blood, yin or yang.

Vacuity heat: Heat due to hyperactive yang in turn due to insufficient controlling yin.

Vessels: The main routes for the distribution of qi and blood, but mainly blood.

Viscera: The solid yin organs of Chinese medicine.

Yin: In the body, substance and nourishment.

Yin vacuity: Insufficient yin substance necessary to nourish, control and counterbalance yang activity.

Yang: In the body, function, movement, activity, transformation.

Yang vacuity: Insufficient warming and transforming function giving rise to symptoms of cold in the body.

INDEX